New

Children's Illustrated History

O.L. Henderson
Richard Ward

CLASS 5

OXFORD
UNIVERSITY PRESS

OXFORD
UNIVERSITY PRESS

YMCA Library Building, Jai Singh Road, New Delhi 110001

Oxford University Press is a department of the University of Oxford.
It furthers the University's objective of excellence in research, scholarship,
and education by publishing worldwide in

Oxford New York
Auckland Cape Town Dar es Salaam Hong Kong Karachi
Kuala Lumpur Madrid Melbourne Mexico City Nairobi
New Delhi Shanghai Taipei Toronto

With offices in
Argentina Austria Brazil Chile Czech Republic France Greece
Guatemala Hungary Italy Japan Poland Portugal Singapore
South Korea Switzerland Thailand Turkey Ukraine Vietnam

Published in India
by Oxford University Press

First published as *A Children's Illustrated History*, 1977
Revised as *New Children's Illustrated History*, 1997
Third edition 2007
Fifth impression 2009

ISBN-13: 978-0-19-568386-8
ISBN-10: 0-19-568386-2

Illustrations by Kallol Majumder

Typeset in Aldine BT 401
by Bukprint, Delhi
Printed in India by Universal Offset, Delhi 110092
and published by Oxford University Press
YMCA Library Building, Jai Singh Road, New Delhi 110001

Preface

There is general agreement among historians and history teachers in favour of creating a background of world history before children are introduced to the history of their own country. This gives students a sense of continuity when they study the history of their own people. This book is the first in a series of three books on world history for the Junior School. This preliminary course aims at introducing the child to the various phases of historical development beginning with the earliest civilizations.

This new edition has been thoroughly revised taking into account the feedback given by teachers. Many new elements have been added. The concept of **timelines** gives the children an idea of the time frame and brings events into perspective. Most of the chapters now have **maps** to give the children a sense of the geographical locations. **New topics and chapters** have been included to make it more current and up-to-date. **Did you knows** add interest. The activity section includes interactive and exciting **things to do** which will develop the children's interest in history.

The book for Class 3 begins with an introduction to history and concludes with the death of Julius Caesar. Class 4 begins with a chapter on Jesus Christ and takes the child up to the eighteenth century. In Class 5 the child is introduced to the American War of Independence and ends with the achievements of Nelson Mandela. The three books take the child from the past to the present. Each chapter is in the form of a story or a simple narrative told interestingly. Both biographical and culture-epoch methods have been used. The heroes of war and peace find their place in the former method while the latter approach highlights important historical events and processes. The chapters are arranged chronologically with timelines given at the beginning. The children are made aware of the development of writing, town planning, states, empires and religions. At all times the level of understanding displayed by the children in that particular age-group has been kept in mind.

The photographs and illustrations have been chosen, as far as possible, from contemporary or traditional sources rather than from fanciful reconstruction. Children are introduced to sources of history when they try to relate these materials to the findings of historians. The exercises reinforce learning. Words to remember at the beginning of each chapter draw attention to new ideas or concepts introduced in the chapter as well as to words that might be unfamiliar to the child.

Contents

1. George Washington—The first US president 5
2. Tipu Sultan—The tiger of Mysore 13
3. Napoleon—The hero of the French people 20
4. Simon Bolivar—The great liberator of South America 29
5. Abraham Lincoln—The man who freed the slaves 37
6. Florence Nightingale—The lady with the lamp 45
7. Laxmibai—The brave Rani of Jhansi 53
8. Rabindranath Tagore—India's first Nobel Prize winner 60

Unit Test 1 66

9. Mahatma Gandhi—The father of the nation 67
10. Lenin—The Russian Bolshevik leader 75
11. Sir Winston Churchill—The great statesman 83
12. Sarojini Naidu—The nightingale of India 91
13. Mao Tse-tung—The Chinese Communist leader 97
14. J.R.D. Tata—The father of modern Indian industry 105
15. Mother Teresa—The angel of mercy 112
16. Nelson Mandela—The man who battled apartheid 118

Unit Test 2 124

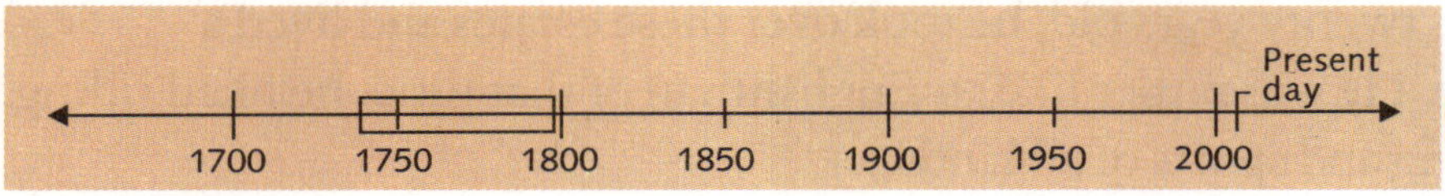

George Washington

—The first US President

George Washington was born in Virginia in USA in 1732. He became the first President of the United States and was known as the Father of the Nation.

George Washington was the descendant of a rich family which came from Britain. His family, like many other British and European families, had made the voyage to America about the middle of the seventeenth century. They had large **estates** in America, where they grew tobacco. When George

George Washington

Words to remember

estates : pieces of property in the form of land.

infantry : soldiers who fight on foot.

cavalry : soldiers fighting on horses, elephants or armoured vehicles.

representatives : persons chosen or elected to speak and act on behalf of others.

achievements : things done successfully with effort and skill.

Congress : a formal meeting for discussion between representatives; (today) governing body that makes laws, especially that of the USA.

Washington was twenty years old, he took over these estates and lived a comfortable life. He was rather like an Englishman of that time; he liked riding, shooting, hunting and sports of all kinds.

At that time, a war broke out between France and Britain. One of the reasons was the struggle for supremacy in America. George Washington left his country estates and joined the British forces. He was a very successful soldier and a good horseman. He soon earned a name for himself as a brilliant officer.

During the war, George Washington served under General Braddock. Braddock was not young and his ideas were very old-fashioned. He wanted to continue to fight battles as soldiers had done for hundreds of years before him. Washington, on the other hand, was full of new ideas. He wanted to make use of Native American scouts, because they were good horsemen and clever at living in the forests. Braddock did not agree.

In those days, the uniform of the British soldiers was red, with plenty of brass buttons and buckles. Washington realized that soldiers dressed like this could easily be seen from a long distance. Washington was proved right. A force of British troops, **infantry** and **cavalry**, was on the march. Unfortunately for them they had been noticed by some French soldiers. The French carefully hid behind the trees and rocks. As the British came past, the French attacked them fiercely. Within a few minutes, half the British soldiers lay dead on the ground. Washington himself escaped, but his horse was shot.

Washington managed to catch another horse which was galloping by without a rider. In a few minutes this horse, too, was shot. At last, on a third horse, he managed to escape; when he got back to his camp, he discovered a number of bullet holes in his clothes.

At last the British and the French made peace with each other. Washington, now a famous officer, left the army and went back to his estates in Virginia. He married a rich widow and spent his time in making his estates as fine as any in the whole of Virginia. Soon he became very wealthy.

Unfortunately, he was not allowed to live comfortably and quietly on his estates. Another war started, which we now know as the American War of Independence.

Many people living in America at the time had come from Britain. Britain considered America to be one of her colonies. It had kept an army in America. The Parliament in Britain made the Americans pay tax on several things. The Americans soon found that Britain was more interested in getting money from America than in spending it there. The Americans began to complain. They said that they had no **representatives** in the Parliament in Britain and hence, the British Parliament had no right to take tax from them. The Americans were particularly angry because Britain put a heavy tax on tea.

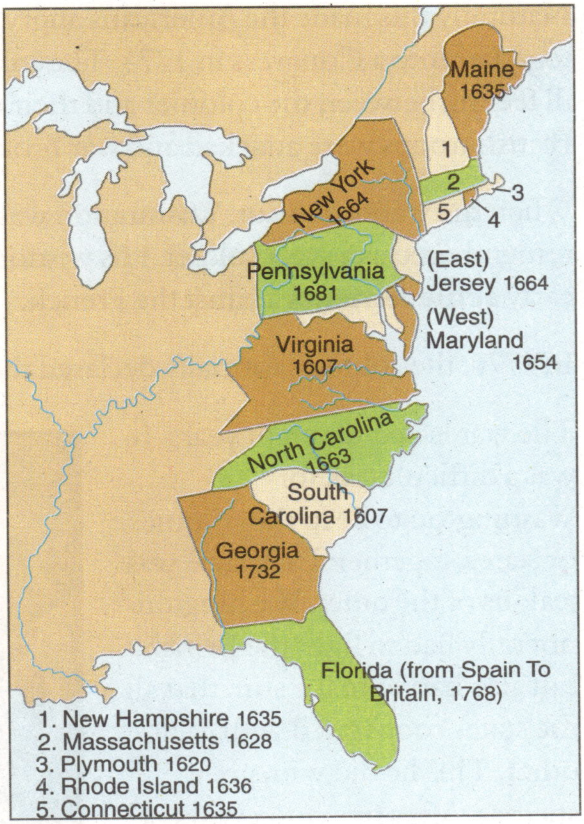

The thirteen colonies

In 1773, some ships carrying tea arrived in Boston harbour. Some Americans dressed up as Native Americans, went on board the ship and threw all the tea into the sea. This was afterwards known as the Boston Tea Party, and it made the British Government very angry. They wanted to punish the Americans and told the colony of Massachusetts that they would not have the right to govern as they had been doing.

The Boston Tea Party

Naturally this made the Americans angry, too, and thirteen colonies joined together into a Congress in 1774. They all agreed not to trade with Britain. The ill feeling between the colonies and their masters grew worse. In 1775, some British troops were attacked and war broke out.

When the war broke out, Washington was in his estates in Virginia. He was still remembered as a great soldier. His wisdom and bravery was known through his early **achievements** against the French.

In 1776, the colonies formally declared themselves independent.

George Washington in battle

The war lasted for eight years. It was a difficult task for Washington to keep the colonies, or states, together. Each state was jealous of the other. Washington not only had to fight the British, but also had to make sure that all the states cooperated with each other. This he did with great success. After five or six years of war, Washington was still fighting, but every day things became more difficult for him. It was not easy to get men for his army and he could only get farmers and other workers to join his army. It was difficult to maintain discipline. The soldiers were badly clothed and poorly fed and it was often impossible to pay them. Washington realized that it would be very difficult to beat the British with such soldiers, so he tried to wear down the British by attacking them at a number of places at the same time. At last a famous British commander called General Cornwallis made his headquarters in Virginia, at a place called Yorktown. Washington had made friends with the French, and the French attacked the British with their troops and prevented them from bringing in stores and equipment. General Cornwallis had to surrender and this was the end of the war.

Peace was signed in 1783, and once more Washington returned home to Virginia. But when the war was over, the states began to quarrel among themselves. One or two wiser statesmen realized that if these quarrels went on, there might be thirteen different countries. They knew that if the thirteen states united into one country they would be stronger and would also be able to help one another prosper. They needed one government for all the states. So Washington was called from Virginia. He presided over a Conference at Philadelphia in 1787, where a new constitution was framed. In 1789, he was made the first President of the United States.

The surrender of General Cornwallis

There were many difficulties in the early years. The states still quarrelled amongst themselves. Some people felt that if there was one President he would be too powerful. He would be like a dictator. Other people felt that it would be difficult for one central government to look after all the states fairly.

The Conference at Philadelphia

Washington was first asked to be President in 1789 for four years. He realized that America was a new country. He knew that it had no traditions or customs which could be followed, and that he would have to make new rules and set up a good government. He introduced a number of ceremonies. He wanted people to think that the President was an important and dignified person. For example, he used to drive to **Congress** in a fine coach, which was always drawn by white horses. He held grand parties. But at the same time, he kept the states together.

He made new laws about owning land and refused to fight on either side in the wars which started between France and England.

Washington was asked to serve as the President for a second term of four years. Then he found that two separate parties were being formed in the Congress. One party was called the Federalist Party. They were led by a man called Hamilton. They thought that the government should be a central one and that the states should be bound by all the rules of the centre. The second party was called the Republican Party. They were led by a man called Jefferson. They wanted the states to have more power than the centre. Washington tried to bring these two parties together, but he was attacked by the Republicans. Washington then went over to the side of the Federalists.

After his second term of four years, people wanted him to serve for another term, but he refused and went back to his estates in Virginia.

The Americans, in the years that followed, respected him more and more, and he has gone down in history as the man who was 'first in war, first in peace and first in the hearts of his countrymen'.

Did you know?

Many places are named after George Washington including the US capital, a state, 31 counties and 17 communities.

Exercises

1. Answer the following.

(a) Why did the French and British fight with each other in America? On whose side did George Washington fight? Why?

(b) What changes did Washington suggest to General Braddock regarding warfare?

(c) Why did the Americans want to break away from Britain and refuse to pay the taxes?

(d) Why was it decided to have one government to govern the thirteen states?
(e) What were the different things George Washington did when he was elected President for the first time?
(f) Which were the two parties of the United States of America? Why could these two parties of the Congress not agree with each other?
(g) How is George Washington remembered in history?

2. **Fill in the blanks.**
(a) George Washington was born in the year .... in ....
(b) He became the first .... of the United States of America.
(c) Tea was thrown into the sea at .... by the .... who dressed as ....
(d) In 1776 the .... declared themselves independent.
(e) A new constitution was framed at .... in ....

3. **Say whether the following are True or False.**
(a) George Washington was the descendant of a rich family in Africa.
(b) In the eighteenth century, the uniform of the British soldiers was red, with plenty of brass buttons and buckles.
(c) Washington was first asked to be President in 1799 for four years.
(d) After his second term of four years, people wanted Washington to serve for another term, but he refused.
(e) The Republicans wanted the centre to have more power than the states.

Things to do

1. **Map work.**

   On a map of North America colour the thirteen colonies. Also mark on it some of the places mentioned in this chapter.

2. **Find out.**

   Draw a flag of the United States of America in your scrapbook. Find out all the relevant information about the flag and share it in class.

3. **Check out this website for some information about symbols of the United States of America.**

   http://www.apples4theteacher.com/coloring.pages/flag-day-united-states-symbols/index (accessed on 11 August 06)

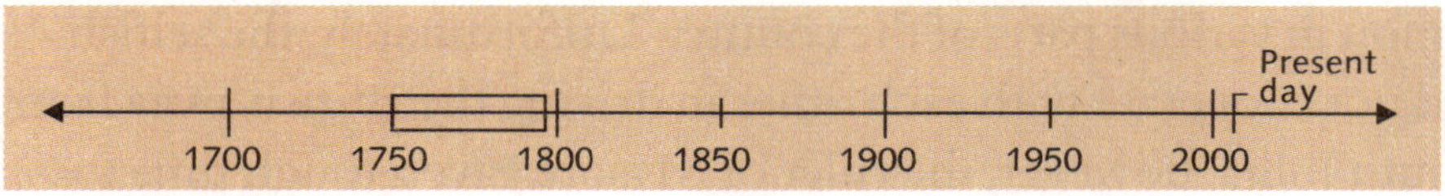

2

Tipu Sultan

—The tiger of Mysore

You have read in class 4 how Vasco da Gama, the Portuguese explorer, discovered a sea route to India in 1498. After this, many European countries like Britain, France, Holland and Denmark began to trade with India by sea. Of these, the British were the most important. They formed a trading company called the East India Company and carried on trade along the coast of India. They built factories in important ports like Bombay, Surat, Madras and Calcutta.

A painting showing the British East India Company's fort at Madras

India, then, was divided into many states under different independent rulers. These rulers were not very friendly with each other. The British took advantage of this and wanted to bring these states under their control. Slowly by 1760, they set up

Words to remember

dynasty : a series of rulers all belonging to the same family.
peasants : poor farmers who worked on the farms of large landowners.
gallantly : bravely.
ignorant : knowing little; being unaware.
barbarian : uncivilized.
struggle : fight.

their administration in various parts of the country. Unfortunately, the selfish Indian rulers did not cooperate with each other in driving the British away from their land. In South India, however, the ruler of Mysore gave a tough time to the British.

At this time, Mysore was ruled by a very brave and able king. His name was Tipu Sultan. He was born in 1753. His father, Hyder Ali, who was also a very able man, had founded a Muslim **dynasty** in Mysore in 1763. Before Hyder became the ruler, Mysore was a Hindu state under a Hindu Raja.

Tipu Sultan

While Tipu was still a boy, his father became the Sultan of Mysore. Tipu was taught the art of fighting at a very young age. He was also educated well and was taught to speak Persian fluently, as it was the court language. Hyder Ali was keen to make his son a good soldier because Mysore at that time was surrounded by a number of enemy states. In the north, the Marathas were a powerful race who were expanding their territories on all sides. Then there was a Nizam, the ruler of Hyderabad (modern Andhra Pradesh), a cunning man who had his eyes on the northern part of Mysore. Besides these Indian enemy states, the ruler of Mysore had one more powerful and dangerous enemy, the British. In the Deccan, the British had set up their power in Bombay and Madras. The states of Carnatic and Travancore were also on friendly terms with the British.

With so many enemies around him, Hyder Ali had to fight two important wars against the British. Besides the British, another foreign power, the French, had also settled in some parts of India. The British and the French were not friendly with each other. During the second war, Hyder Ali took the help of the French to fight against the British. Tipu also helped his father and defeated the British army in 1782. In the same year, when the war was still going on, Hyder Ali died, leaving his son Tipu to continue the struggle. Hyder Ali's death pleased the

British as they thought they had got rid of a dangerous enemy. But they soon realized that the new ruler of Mysore was a more dangerous enemy to fight against. Meanwhile, the French had to withdraw their help to Mysore. This was a big blow to Tipu but it did not discourage him completely. He fought on single-handed. At last when the British saw what a brave soldier Tipu was, they decided to make peace with him. The two sides signed a treaty and the war came to an end.

Tipu used the next few years to strengthen his own kingdom. He assumed the title *Padshah*, which means emperor. He proved to be an efficient ruler. He made a number of improvements in the government and made new laws for the collection of taxes. He protected the **peasants** and even rewarded them for their services. He tried to get rid of the moneylenders. Many of the Englishmen who visited his kingdom praised his administration. He was very popular among his subjects. Though he was a Muslim, he did not force his Hindu subjects to follow Islam.

Tipu was an ambitious man and wanted to increase his territory. He wanted to take over Travancore, a state to the south of Mysore, and attacked it in 1789. The Raja of this state was under the protection of the British. The British now hurriedly came to help the Raja. The Nizam of Hyderabad and the Marathas also joined the British to destroy the power of the brave Tipu.

Tipu tried to get help from the French, but France was at that time going through a great revolution (about which you will read in Chapter 3) and so the French could not give him any help. In 1790, the British, the Marathas and the Nizam attacked Mysore. The war continued for two years and Tipu could no longer fight alone. He signed a treaty in 1792 and the war came to an end. Tipu had to give away half of his kingdom to the victorious armies. Thus, the British gained control of the whole of the western coast of Mysore. The Marathas and the Nizam also got their share of the territory in the north of Mysore.

Although Tipu lost a great deal of his kingdom, he was not discouraged. In the next six years, he was able to improve his military power and financial position. He sent his men to Mauritius, which was under the French, and tried to get

The Partition of Mysore in 1799

help from them. The French promised help this time. A few Frenchmen joined Tipu's army and also gave military training to his soldiers. At that time, Tipu heard that Napoleon of France (about whom you will read in Chapter 3) had invaded Egypt. He hoped that Napoleon's forces would march through Egypt to India and drive the British out of the country. Unfortunately for Tipu, the government in Britain also realized the possibility of French forces invading India from Egypt. They sent a very able Englishman to India to deal with this danger.

Lord Wellesley

In 1798, Lord Wellesley came to India as the new Governor-General of the British colonies in this country. He was a brave general and was determined to completely crush the power of Tipu Sultan. Wellesley wanted to defeat Tipu before Napoleon's forces came to India. He sought the help of the Marathas and the Nizam of Hyderabad and once again these two enemy states willingly agreed to help the British. The unfortunate Sultan of Mysore was thus left to fight all alone against the three powerful enemies. The little French help that he got was not of much use and Napoleon's plan of invading India failed. In 1799, Tipu died **gallantly** defending his capital, Seringapatam, against the enemy.

The siege of Seringapatam

With Tipu's death, the British got rid of one of their most dangerous and dreaded enemies. His kingdom was divided among the British, the Marathas and the Nizam. The British took most of the territory. The Muslim rule in Mysore came to an end. A Hindu Raja who was completely under the power of the British, was put on the throne of Mysore.

Tipu's last battle

Tipu ruled Mysore for seventeen years (1782–99). During this time, he was a 'constant source of alarm and danger' to the British. They feared and hated him. That is why many British writers of those times have described Tipu in unfair terms. They have called him '**ignorant**' and 'a mad **barbarian**'. But these are one-sided opinions. The fact is that Tipu was neither ignorant nor mad. He was an efficient ruler and a brave general. He was well educated, which is proved by the fact that he had a huge library. He took a deep interest in administration and wrote the orders to his men in his own hand. Tipu Sultan loved his country. He believed in independence. That is why he could never accept British overlordship. Tipu Sultan, the tiger of Mysore, is remembered as a great figure in the history of India's **struggle** against the British.

Did you know?

Like his father Hyder Ali, Tipu Sultan also used rocket weapons and improvised them. Dr A.P.J. Abdul Kalam, in his Tipu Sultan Shaheed Memorial lecture in 1991, called Tipu the innovator of the world's first war rocket.

Exercises

1. Answer the following.

(a) Who were the enemies of Tipu on his northern frontiers?
(b) Why did the French help Hyder Ali?
(c) Was Tipu a good ruler? How did he help the peasants?
(d) How did the British writers describe Tipu?
(e) Write a sentence on each of the following dates:
• 1782 • 1790 • 1792

2. Fill in the blanks.

(a) Tipu Sultan was born in ....
(b) The states of .... and .... were friendly with the British.
(c) Tipu was taught to speak .... fluently.
(d) Tipu assumed the name of ...., which means ....
(e) Tipu attacked .... in 1789.

3. **Say whether the following are True or False.**
   (a) Before Hyder Ali became the ruler, Mysore was a Muslim state under a Muslim ruler.
   (b) The Nizam of Hyderabad and the Marathas helped Tipu to destroy the power of the British.
   (c) In 1789, Lord Wellesley came to India as the new Governor-General of the British colonies.
   (d) In 1799, Tipu died gallantly defending Mysore, against the enemy.
   (e) Tipu Sultan, is known as the tiger of Mysore.

Things to do

1. **Solve the puzzle given below.**

Down

1. The Governor-General who came to India in 1798
2. Tipu's father
3. Powerful neighbours north of Tipu's kingdom

Across

4. Tipu's capital
5. The ruler of Hyderabad
6. The name of the trading company set up by the British

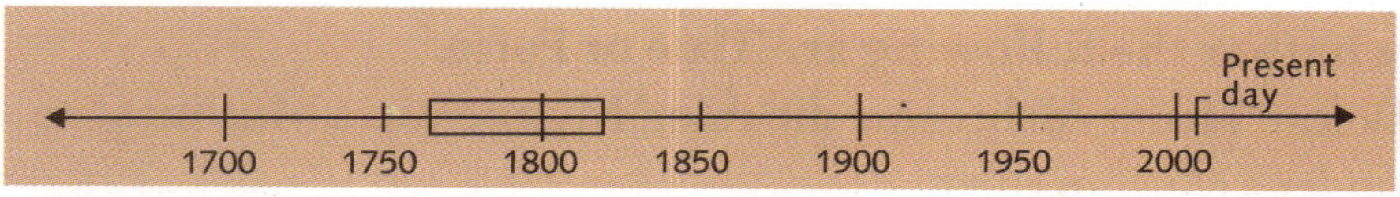

Napoleon

—The hero of the French people

The story of Napoleon is one of the great adventure stories in the history of modern Europe. Napoleon was born in 1769 in Corsica, a small island in the Mediterranean Sea. This island had been independent at one time but when Napoleon was born, it had already been conquered by France. Napoleon's father worked for the French government, and after ten years the government allowed him to send his son to France to be educated. Napoleon was sent to a military school, because he had always wanted to be a soldier. He

Napoleon

Words to remember

luxury : a state of life in which a person uses expensive things (which are not essential) for the sake of pleasure.

republic : a system of government in which the representatives are elected.

distress : a feeling of great worry or unhappiness; suffering.

regime : a system of administration.

humble : showing you do not think that you are as important as other people; low in rank (in context, only this).

abandoned : left and no longer wanted, used or needed.

allies : a group of countries fighting on the same side in war.

was a short, stout boy. Although he spoke French well, he spoke it with a foreign accent and all the boys laughed at him.

'Look at Napoleon!' they shouted. 'See how short he is!'

'And stout too,' shouted another boy.

'Not only that. Listen to the way he speaks. He can't even speak French properly,' cried a third.

'Oh, well, you're only a foreigner. Why don't you go back to Corsica?'

Napoleon knew that soldiers should not cry, so he put on a brave face and buried his head in his books. He had a wonderful memory and he read all the books he could find about soldiers and armies and battles fought long ago. At the age of fifteen, he became an officer in the French army.

Louis XVI

At that time France was being very badly governed. The laws were not fair, and the poor people were taxed very heavily. The king, Louis XVI, was so powerful that he could do what he liked. The king and his rich nobles lived in great **luxury** and were ignorant of the wretched conditions of the people. It is said, one day, when the queen heard that the people were starving and did not even have bread to eat, she remarked—'If they don't have bread, why don't they eat cake?' The king did nothing to put these things right. So, finally, a terrible revolution broke out. On 14 July 1789, hundreds of people in Paris revolted and attacked a famous prison called the Bastille, where prisoners whom the king did not like were kept. During the next few years, both the king and the queen and many nobles were killed. The ordinary people of France set up a **republic**. Their cry was—'Liberty, Equality, Fraternity'.

Liberty means freedom for everybody. **Equality** means that all are equal and **fraternity** means that men should treat each other as brothers.

The storming of the Bastille

But the new leaders did not know how to rule and quarrelled with one another and France was in great **distress**. The kings in the countries around France, especially Prussia and Austria, were afraid that the revolution in France might spread to their countries; so they attacked France in order to stop the revolution.

Napoleon, who was still quite young, welcomed the revolution with great delight. He thought that the revolution opened up great opportunities for an ambitious man like him. Under the old **regime**, where the king and his rich nobles ruled the country, he could not have risen to a high position in the army because of his **humble** background. Napoleon, who was already known to be an officer of genius, was just the man that France needed. He was promoted and given command of an army to fight against the Austrians.

Josephine

Just before leaving Paris, Napoleon met Josephine, a rich and beautiful young woman, and married her. She later introduced Napoleon to many rich people who could help him.

In Europe, Napoleon was victorious everywhere. He was very successful in commanding his men and soon showed that he was a brilliant general. He was able to march his men very quickly from place to place. He did not follow the usual rules of battles. He always attacked the enemy wherever and whenever they were least expected. In those days, as in the days of Babur and Alexander, both armies lined up opposite each other and prepared for the battle. When one of the armies charged against the other, the battle used to start. Napoleon did not follow these rules at all. He first showed himself with his army, in front of the enemy; then, before they realized what was happening, he would take his men and horses very quickly in the opposite direction and attacked the enemy in the rear. Also, when he attacked, he would hold back some troops in reserve and then, when both sides would get tired, he would suddenly throw these fresh troops into the battle.

When Napoleon came to Paris he found that everyone knew his name. He was well known, and in later years, was known as one of the world's most famous generals. He became the terror of Europe and the hero of the French people.

Napoleon in Egypt

At that time France was at war with Britain. Britain was trying to help the ex-rulers of France. Britain not only fought the French on land, but also had a great fleet of fighting ships. These ships were commanded by a famous admiral called Nelson. Napoleon saw that Britain's strength was her Mediterranean and Eastern trade. He decided to attack Egypt to prevent the British from carrying on trade with India so that India would be within his grasp. 'This little Europe,' he said, 'is too small a field. Real fame can only be won in the East.' Nelson at that time had his fleet in the Mediterranean, but Napoleon managed to get into Egypt before Nelson's ships could catch him. But when he had defeated the Egyptians, Napoleon found that Nelson had set fire to all his ships. This upset his plans to go to the East.

Napoleon left his army in Egypt and managed to return to France. France was then a discontented country. The people had set up a new kind of government which was not working very well. Napoleon and some others took over the government and Napoleon became the leader. He was made the First Consul and later, in 1804, he was made the emperor. As soon as he took over the government, Napoleon showed what a genius he was. He made many changes in the country. He appointed people from Paris to go to various parts of the country and to govern the people, but each of these governors was still responsible to him. He controlled the whole country from Paris; he introduced new taxes and started a national bank. He made the Catholic religion the official religion of the country.

Then he invited the Pope to come from Rome to crown him emperor. All the important people of Paris and all the governors of the provinces were present there. Napoleon was in his uniform with his medals and sword, and he carried his own crown. But when the Pope reached out his hands to take the crown, in order to put it on Napoleon's head, Napoleon put it on his own head and crowned himself! He then crowned Josephine as the empress.

Did you know?

Napoleon gave to the nation the Code Napoleon. It was the first clear, compact statement of French law in centuries. It became a model for law reformers throughout the world.

By 1807, Napoleon's armies had taken over nearly the whole of Europe. He had also tried to make friends with Russia, and hoped that Russia would do whatever he wanted; the only country left to conquer was Britain.

A bitter struggle followed. Many people in Britain thought that Napoleon would bring his armies across the English Channel and invade Britain. Napoleon found this impossible, but he used his navy to blockade Britain. This meant that he tried to stop ships from bringing food to Britain from across the seas. British did not grow enough food to feed herself and Napoleon thought

The French Empire under Napoleon

that if he could stop food from coming into the country, the people of Britain would starve. There were many sea battles between the British and the French. The British also attacked France through Spain and Portugal, and at last, Napoleon realized that he would have to defeat the Russians before anything, as the Russian emperor had shown himself less and less inclined to be a trusted partner of Napoleon.

Napoleon set out against Russia with an army of more than 4,50,000 men.

The Russians retreated because they knew their army could never match Napoleon's. Napoleon advanced many hundreds of miles and the Russians avoided a battle and retreated. At last he attacked the Russians, but in doing so, he lost thousands of his soldiers, many more than he had expected. He marched on to Moscow and found the whole city empty as the Russians had **abandoned** it. The Russians abandoned the villages and even destroyed them so that Napoleon could get no food from the villagers. Napoleon realized that he would have to return to France, and started the long journey home. It was winter and bitterly cold. The snow lay thick on the ground as Napoleon and his men marched home towards France. The wounded were left to die in the snow. There was hardly any food and many of the soldiers died of starvation. At last Napoleon and his small army struggled back to France; there were fewer than 10,000 left out of the 4,50,000 who had started out for Russia.

Napoleon and his army retreating from Russia

This disaster encouraged all the people of Europe to defy Napoleon and he was defeated at a great battle fought near a place called Leipzig. Finally, in March 1814, the English armies entered Paris and Napoleon was taken prisoner. A new king, Louis XVIII, was crowned, and Napoleon was sent as a prisoner to the tiny island of Elba, between Corsica and Italy.

A year later, he escaped. He managed to collect a thousand soldiers and marched into France. Very soon they met the army of the king, and Napoleon realized that his thousand men would soon be defeated. He rode forward to meet the commander of the king's army. The two horses stopped within a few yards of each other.

'Do you know who I am?' asked Napoleon.

'I do indeed,' replied the general. 'You are Napoleon Bonaparte. You have just escaped from Elba and I command you to surrender in the name of the king.'

'We shall not surrender,' said Napoleon. 'Do you remember that I was once your emperor? If there is one soldier in your army who wants to kill his emperor, let him stand forth.'

The Battle of Waterloo

Napoleon threw his arms wide open.

'Here I am,' he said. 'Kill me if you dare!'

A cheer went up from the men of the king's army and within minutes, they joined Napoleon and marched towards Paris.

And so Napoleon returned. But he was soon defeated at the Battle of Waterloo by a famous British general called the Duke of Wellington in 1815.

After this battle Napoleon was imprisoned on another island called St Helena, and six years later, he died there. He was one of the greatest soldiers the world has ever seen.

Exercises

1. Answer the following.

(a) What was the cry of the common people of France who wanted to set up a republic?
(b) In what ways was Napoleon a good general?
(c) Why did Napoleon attack Egypt? What happened there?
(d) What did Napoleon do when he became the emperor?
(e) Describe Napoleon's war with Russia.

2. **Fill in the blanks.**

(a) Napoleon was born in .... on the island of ....

(b) The people of Paris revolted in 1789 and attacked the prison called ....

(c) In later years, Napoleon became the world's most famous .... and the .... of Europe.

(d) Napoleon invited the .... to crown him emperor.

(e) Napoleon was sent as a prisoner to .... in the year 1814.

(f) After the Battle of .... Napoleon was imprisoned at.............................. .

3. **Match the following.**

(a) Duke of Wellington	King of France
(b) Nelson	British general
(c) Catholic	British admiral
(d) Louis XVIII	Official religion of France

Things to do

1. **For your scrapbook.**

Stick pictures of Nelson and Napoleon in your book.

2. **Map work.**

On an outline map of Europe mark Italy, Corsica, Spain, London and Paris. Can you find Elba and St Helena?

3. **Check the following website.**

http://www.napoleonbonaparte.nl/ (accessed on 11 August 06)

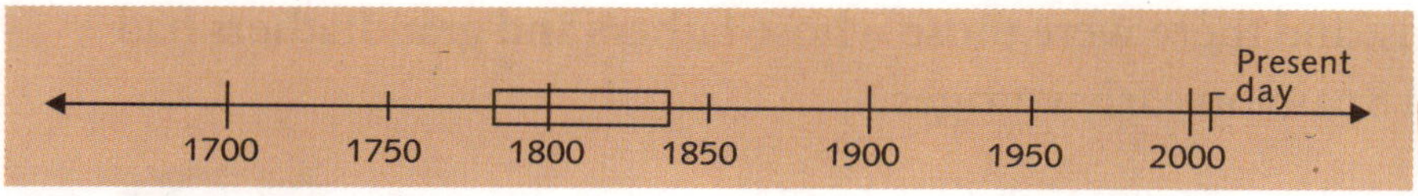

Simon Bolivar

—The great liberator of South America

Just as George Washington is honoured as the Father of the Nation in the United States, the name of Simon Bolivar is linked with freedom in South America. Simon Bolivar was born in Venezuela in 1783.

Simon Bolivar

Venezuela is a large country in the northern part of South America. At that time, most of South America belonged to Spain. Many years before, Spain had sent her sailors and armies across the Atlantic Ocean and settled in many parts of South America. These countries were ruled from Spain and faced the same problems as the American colonies had faced in the United States. The government in Spain ruled them very sternly. They would not allow them to have any part in their own government. In addition, the people of Spain looked down on the people of their colonies. In Venezuela, there were two groups of people. There were the original **inhabitants** of the country, Native

Words to remember

inhabitants : people living in a place.
devil : evil being; a wicked spirit.
glinted : shone with light.
unceasing : not stopping.
torrents : great downpour of rain.
endured : suffered something painful or uncomfortable patiently.

South Americans, and there were those whose fathers and grandfathers had come over from Spain on early voyages.

Simon Bolivar was born into a rich family. His parents had come from Spain and had settled down in Venezuela, but they died when he was a child. Bolivar was taught at home by tutors, and he remembered one of them, particularly, all his life. The tutor's name was Rodriguez. Rodriguez gave Bolivar many books to read, but the most important books were about freedom. Bolivar had many talks with his teacher about freedom.

Rodriguez

'If others in the world are free,' asked Bolivar, 'what about us?'

'The people of Venezuela will never be free,' said Rodriguez.

'Why not?' asked Bolivar.

'Because of the Spaniards,' replied his teacher. 'Spain rules us cruelly. They think that we are people of the **devil** and that they have been created by God. They take our riches and give us nothing in return. Who knows when we shall be liberated from their rule?'

'What does liberated mean?' asked Bolivar.

'It means to be free,' said his tutor. 'Free to rule ourselves.'

'When I grow up,' said Bolivar, 'I shall do nothing else except work for that freedom.'

When he was sixteen, Bolivar went to Spain. He wanted to study law. He thought this would be useful in his future struggle for freedom. There were no universities in Venezuela at that time and as Bolivar was rich, he could afford to travel to Spain. He went to Madrid, the capital of Spain, which was a very beautiful city. Bolivar enjoyed the life in Madrid, but he also worked hard and read as much as he could. In 1802, he married a beautiful girl who was the daughter of a Spanish nobleman. He was nineteen then, and he took her back to South America with him. But after a year, she caught fever and died.

South America

Bolivar went back to Europe where he met his old friend and teacher, Rodriguez. In the years after the French Revolution, the Spanish king had been defeated by Napoleon. The people of Venezuela decided to revolt, and they broke away from Spain and set up their own government. However, after Napoleon was defeated, the king of Spain came back to his throne and the Spaniards overcame the people of Venezuela and once more took over the country. Soon after this there was a terrible earthquake in Venezuela. The Spanish nobles called the Venezuelan leaders to a great meeting. One of them addressed the meeting:

'A little while ago,' he said, 'you were foolish. You thought that our good Spanish rule was over. You were happy when the King of Spain was driven out of our country by Napoleon. You foolishly thought you could take over the government.' The Venezuelan leaders continued to listen, but their faces were sad.

'Now we have come,' said the nobleman, 'to rule again. And what has happened? God has sent you a terrible punishment. He has made the earth open and your towns and villages have disappeared and many of your people have been killed. This is your punishment, the earthquake. This is the punishment God has sent you for trying to overthrow Spain.'

Bolivar was now back in Venezuela. On the way, he had visited the United

States. He admired the Americans, and he particularly admired George Washington, who had fought so bravely for independence. Bolivar collected round him as many men as he could. They were all men who wanted to free the country from the rule of Spain. Some of them came from Colombia, the country next door, to Venezuela.

Although he had only six or seven hundred men and he was not an experienced soldier, Bolivar led his little army into the town of Caracas. He managed to defeat the Spaniards and drive them out of the town. Bolivar was pleased with his first success and even more pleased when the cheering crowds called him 'Liberator'. But he knew that his little army could not stand up to the strength of Spain. In a few months, Spain had collected an army, and not only drove him out of Caracas but out of the country altogether. He had no money and most of his soldiers had been killed.

Bolivar had to leave South America, and he went to Jamaica in the West Indies. He had to live in Jamaica with the poorest of the poor. He lived in a small hut and spent his time thinking of a plan for making Venezuela free from Spanish rule. He started writing some of his ideas about freedom. Some of these writings were sent to Europe. He wanted to unite all the countries in South America. He did not want a dictator or a king; he wanted a democracy, like the government of Britain.

In the West Indies, Bolivar spent a long time in planning what he would do when he got back to Venezuela. Even while he was in Jamaica, the Spaniards tried to kill him. He and a friend shared a small hut. Bolivar always slept on the right of the door near the window. His friend slept at the other side of the hut. One evening, Bolivar said to his friend:

'I am going out this evening. I promised to meet some friends who may be able to help us in getting some money.'

'Where are you going?' asked his friend.

'To Kuta,' said Bolivar. 'It is about ten miles from here. I shan't be back until tomorrow. I must see them; they are going away in a few days. They are rich and they hate the Spanish. If I can get some money we can gather together a few men and perhaps start our work again.'

The friend agreed and Bolivar said goodbye and walked off into the mountains. He met his friends and pleaded with them until late into the night. They did not believe that if they gave him money he would be able to find an army to conquer the Spaniards. It was with a heavy heart that Bolivar returned the next day to his hut by the river. As he approached it, he called out his friend's name, but there was no reply. Bolivar walked up to the door and opened it wide, calling out his friend's name again. He saw his friend lying across the bed on his stomach. A Spanish dagger **glinted** between his shoulder blades. Bolivar knelt down by the side of the dead body. The poor man had changed his sleeping place, and had gone to sleep in Bolivar's bed. Bolivar knew that the dagger had been meant for him and not for his friend. He never discovered why his friend had moved from his own bed to his, but it was lucky for Bolivar and for Venezuela that he did.

Bolivar still went on looking for friends to help him and at last, he found a good friend in the President of Haiti. Haiti was a republic run by Africans who had liberated their country from French rule. Bolivar managed to find two or three hundred soldiers who were willing to help him, and became the General of one of the smallest armies in the world.

He realized that such a small army would be of no use against the mighty Spanish force. He knew that after the wars in France, between Britain and Napoleon, there would be many soldiers without work. He wrote to his friend in Britain and managed to persuade three thousand soldiers, mostly British and Irish, to cross the Atlantic to join him. These soldiers did not come to fight because they wanted to free Venezuela from the Spaniards; they came for money, and Bolivar promised to pay them well. But the journey across South America was through terrible jungles, and many of these soldiers died. Not many of them arrived safely at Bolivar's camp.

In addition to this, Bolivar found some very useful soldiers among the South American tribesmen. These tribesmen were magnificent horsemen and excellent fighters with their spears. More important, they were used to living in the jungle. Bolivar persuaded them that Spain was ruling over them unjustly, and they agreed to join him.

Bolivar then had an army of six or seven thousand men. With this army he attacked the Spaniards and threw them out of Venezuela. He had meetings with his officers and planned how they would run the country after the Spaniards had left. He made himself President of Venezuela and also President of Colombia.

The Spaniards were still ruling Colombia, and Bolivar thought of a most dangerous and daring plan. He would take his army right over the top of the high Andes Mountains to a town called Bogota, the capital of Colombia, and surprise the Spaniards.

This time his army had to cross some of the most difficult country in the world. He left half his men in Venezuela under the command of a man called Paez and set out with 2,500 men to cross the Andes. It was the rainy season. The rain poured down in **unceasing torrents**. The little army came to huge rivers, which rushed down from the mountains. There were no bridges across these rivers and so Bolivar and his men had to set to work to make boats. They made frames of wood and covered the frames with hides. Then the men and the horses had to struggle across the rushing water. Many men were lost, but still Bolivar struggled on. They had to cross ten rivers before they got to the foot of the Andes. Then the terrible climb began. Men and horses struggled upwards and ever upwards. The weather got colder and colder as they climbed to a height of more than 4,000 metres. Men died of cold, but still Bolivar pushed on. At last they reached the top and after resting for a few days, they went down the other side and marched on to Bogota. Bolivar by then had only 1,000 men left; in front of the city of Bogota was the army of the Spaniards, more than 3,000. But Bolivar and his soldiers had come so far, and had **endured** so much, that they were determined to win. He and his tribesmen fought like tigers and in a very short time, they had defeated the Spaniards and killed most of their soldiers. Bolivar himself was always in the thick of the battle and

Did you know?

Simon Bolivar was known as El Libertador, which means 'The Liberator'. When final Spanish resistance was cleared from an area of Upper Peru, it was renamed Bolivia in his honour.

somehow escaped the Spanish bullets. He was joined by more soldiers and then fought another battle against the Spaniards. On 10 August 1819, they marched into Bogota and liberated Colombia.

A painting depicting the final battle for Peru's independence

Bolivar then went south. He freed all the countries in the south of the continent, Peru, Argentina and Chile, and also the country which is now named after him—Bolivia, which was originally a part of Peru. By 1824, there was no Spanish rule in South America. All the countries had been liberated. But soon they began to quarrel amongst themselves, and Bolivar died in 1830, a disappointed man. At one time he said:

'If my death can contribute anything towards the countries of South America agreeing with each other, I shall go to my grave in peace.'

Today all South Americans remember his name and honour him as the great freedom fighter—'The George Washington of South America'.

Exercises

1. **Answer the following.**
   (a) Why did Bolivar remember his tutor Rodriguez?
   (b) What reasons did the Spanish give for the earthquake?
   (c) How did Bolivar expand his army against the Spanish force?
   (d) What kind of government did Bolivar want to give to his country?
   (e) Why is Bolivar known as 'The George Washington of South America'?

2. **Fill in the blanks.**
   (a) Bolivar went to Spain to study ....
   (b) Bolivar was called the ....
   (c) After Bolivar was driven out of Caracas, he went to
   ....
   (d) Bolivar found a friend in the President of ....
   (e) Bolivar crossed the .... to get to Colombia.

3. **Choose the correct answer.**
   (a) Haiti was a republic run by ....
   i) Africans ii) English iii) Americans iv) Australians
   (b) Bogota is the capital of........... .
   i) Venezuela ii) Colombia iii) Peru iv) Chile
   (c) Bolivar liberated South America from the rule of the
   ....
   i) Spaniards ii) Japanese iii) Chinese iv) Americans
   (d) On 10 August 1819, Bolivar and his army marched into Bogota and liberated ....
   i) Colombia ii) Peru iii) Jamaica iv) Chile

Things to do

1. **Map work.**
   Draw a map of South America. Mark on it all the countries mentioned in this chapter, the main rivers and the Andes Mountains.

2. **Unscramble the letters below to form correct names.**

i. ERPU	....	ii. VARLIBO	....
iii. OGATOB	....	iv. DESAN	....
v. TIAIH	....		

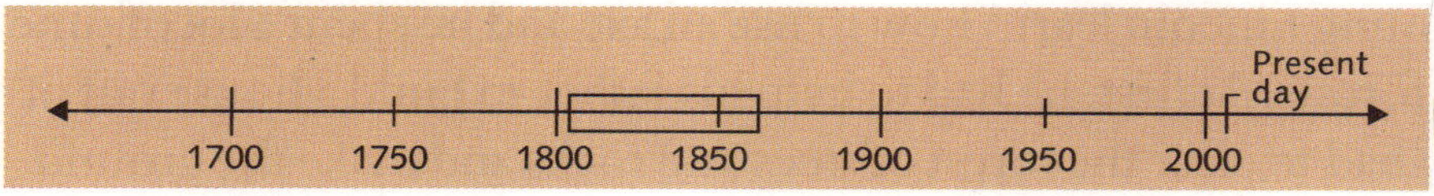

Abraham Lincoln

—The man who freed the slaves

Abraham Lincoln was the sixteenth President of the United States of America. He is chiefly remembered for getting rid of **slavery** and for uniting the States of America.

Abraham Lincoln was born in 1809 on a small farm in Kentucky. He came from a humble background. His father was a farmer. When Abraham Lincoln was eight years old, his father decided to move further west. The whole family took all their possessions with them and arrived in Indiana, which was a state with

Abraham Lincoln

Words to remember

slavery : custom of having slaves; a slave is a person who is the property of another and bound to serve him.
log cabin: cabin with walls made of logs.
shovel: spade-like tool, used for moving coal, sand, etc.
plantation: a large area of land where tea, cotton, sugar cane, etc. are grown.
cell: small room in a prison.
sheriff: chief officer of a district, county or city.
perish: to be lost or destroyed; come to an end.
mourned: regretted; to feel sad.

many forests. Young Lincoln learnt how to use an axe and he spent a lot of time working in the forests. At first, he had to help his father to build a house out of logs. Then they had to clear the forest of trees and rocks and make the ground ready for planting crops. Their chief crop was corn.

Abraham Lincoln was so busy he had no time to go to school. He spent his childhood doing all sorts of jobs like that of a farm labourer, boat-hand, log-chopper and the keeper of a tiny store. He was also a village postmaster for some time and he carried all the letters in his hat. His mother taught him how to read. She inspired him greatly and her advice to him was to 'learn all he could and be of some account in the world'. In the evening after the day's work was over, Abraham liked to spend some time with his books.

When Abraham was a lad of sixteen, he heard that a person living near their house had a book on the life of George Washington. He was very interested in reading it and he begged the owner of the book to lend it to him for a few days. Abraham was given the book, but unfortunately for him, a day later, rain soaked through Abraham's **log cabin** and ruined the book. The poor lad was very upset, as he did not have the money to buy another book and return it to the owner. So Abraham went to the man's farm and offered his free service till the cost of the book was made up. The farmer was so impressed with the young boy's sincerity that when finally Abraham had worked hard enough to make up for the cost of the book, the farmer presented him with the volume. Imagine Abraham's joy when he received this wonderful gift! He had won it through hard labour.

As he often could not afford to buy paper and pencil, Abraham wrote with a piece of chalk and used the **shovel** for an exercise book. Abraham also liked to talk and to argue with his friends. One day he heard the speech of a famous lawyer; Abraham was so delighted that he decided that he, too, would become a lawyer.

When he reached the age of twenty-one, his father sent him on a journey to a town called New Orleans. This was a place nearly two thousand miles away from Abraham's home in Indiana. Abraham and his friend went on the journey together. They got a small boat ready and loaded it with stores and provisions, enough to last them for a long time. They paddled down the Ohio River and then came to the wide Mississippi River.

On their journey Abraham and his friend had many adventures, but what he could never forget was the sight of the slaves. One day Abraham and his friend watched the sale of a Black girl in a slave market. The sight made Abraham sad. Turning to his friend he said, 'Let's get out of here. If I ever get a chance to hit that thing (meaning slavery) I'll hit it hard.'

A cotton plantation under slavery

This was the first time that Abraham came to know about the miserable conditions of the slaves. Abraham had not seen slaves before, and as they passed through the great cotton **plantations**, he saw them working in the fields. Sometimes in the evening, when they stopped their boat at the side of the river, he talked to some of the people who owned them. Although there were one or two slave owners who treated their slaves well, most of them treated their slaves cruelly. The slaves were given no wages, and were forced to work at picking cotton the whole day. They lived in miserable houses, and if they tried to run away, they were cruelly beaten and sometimes even killed. The condition of these slaves made Abraham very sad. He decided that in future he would do what he could to help the slaves in every way and to stop people from using them.

Soon after this, his family moved again, this time to a place called Illinois.

However, Lincoln decided to go and work in New Orleans. He tried a number of different jobs, but finally took up law as a career. Although he had never been to school, he had read a lot of books, and he decided to become a lawyer. In 1837, he passed the examination which allowed him to practise law. He rented a room, put up a board and started work. He was a very good speaker indeed and because he was a good speaker, he won many of his cases. People discovered that he not only worked very hard but that he was also extremely honest. This earned him the nickname of 'Honest Abe'. He was always willing to help the poor, and many stories are told of his kindness.

A print showing the law office of Abraham Lincoln

One day while he was sitting in his office, the jailer of the local jail came to see him.

'We've got a prisoner in our jail, who's just committed a murder,' said the jailer. 'The trial is coming up next week. This man keeps shouting your name. I can't keep him quiet. I want Abe Lincoln, he keeps yelling. So I thought I'd better come and see you.'

'I'll come down to the jail right away,' said Lincoln.

He walked down to the jail. The jailer unlocked the door and Abraham Lincoln stepped into the tiny **cell**. On the bed sat a man. He was a young man but he was so dirty and bearded that he looked much older. He sprang up from the bed as soon as he saw Lincoln.

'You've come!' he cried. 'You're the only man who can save me. Do you remember me? I'm Dave Jackson. We lived in Indiana together.'

‘Of course I do,’ said Lincoln. ‘I remember now that you have told me your name. But you have changed a lot since then. Anyway, why have they put you in here?’

‘My brother was murdered and the **sheriff** says that I did it. You know me well enough, Abe. I would never do a thing like that.’

‘Yes,’ said Lincoln. ‘I know you would not. Tell me all about it.’

A week later, the trial began. Lincoln not only made some fine speeches but he also proved that the Sheriff had made a mistake and that Dave Jackson was not the murderer.

As Lincoln came down the steps of the courthouse, Dave Jackson was released. A woman came out of the crowd carrying her little baby, and rushed into Jackson’s arms. Jackson turned to Lincoln.

‘I owe you a thousand thanks,’ he said, ‘but I’m still in trouble.’

‘What trouble?’ asked Lincoln.

‘I don’t have any money to pay your fee,’ said the man.

‘When I see you and your family so happy,’ said Lincoln, ‘I don’t need any fee.’

At the age of twenty-five, Lincoln was elected to the legislature of Illinois state. This legislature was a meeting place where the laws of the state were decided; members of the legislature were elected or chosen by the people of the state. Thirteen years later, Lincoln won a seat in the Congress, which was the highest assembly in the country. Lincoln was such a good speaker that he soon became very popular. He was also honest and sensible and so people listened to what he said. Lincoln was elected President of the United States in 1860 and soon after this, the Civil War started.

The chief reason for the war was the quarrel about slaves. People in the northern states were opposed to slavery; people in the southern states needed the slaves to work on their cotton plantations. This became the main reason for the quarrel between the North and the South. All the southern states decided to break away from the northern states and form their own country. The southern states said to the northern states, 'You object to slavery; very well, you go your way, and we will go ours.' Lincoln was very much against this, and said that all the states of the union should stay together. In one of his speeches he said, 'A house divided against itself cannot stand.' He was speaking of his country that was divided on a quarrel between the North and South.

At first the southern armies under General Lee won many victories. They slowly defeated the northern forces and marched towards Washington, the capital, in the north. But in 1862, the northern forces, under General Grant, began to fight back much harder and they won a number of important victories. 800,000 people died in the Civil War.

In 1862, while the war was going on, Abraham Lincoln made the most important announcement. As President he declared that from that time onwards all slaves would be freemen. The next year the northern armies won a great victory at a place called Gettysburg. When the men who died at Gettysburg were being buried, Lincoln made a speech. The last sentence of his speech has become famous throughout the world, especially in countries where people think that freedom is important. He said:

> 'We hereby resolve that these dead shall not have died in vain; that this nation, under God, shall have new birth and freedom; and that the government of the people, by the people, for the people, shall not **perish** from the earth.'

At the end of the war, Lincoln managed to carry out what he

Did you know?

Born into poverty, Lincoln was faced with defeat throughout his life. He lost eight elections and twice failed in business. He could have quit many times—but he did not, and went on to become one of the greatest presidents of the USA.

wanted to do most, that is, to get rid of slavery and to keep the North and South together as one country called the United States. He was so popular that he was elected President for the second time. One night, when everybody in Washington was happy that the war was over and that peace had been declared, Lincoln took his wife to the theatre. Suddenly, without any warning, a half-mad man, John Wilkes Booth, appeared in the theatre and shot Lincoln.

The statue of Lincoln at Lincoln Memorial in Washington

Lincoln's death in 1865 was **mourned** by all the people of America. They had hoped that he would continue to lead them for many years, and they were shocked at his death.

Abraham Lincoln personified the values of honesty, integrity, respect for human rights and freedom.

Exercises

1. **Answer the following.**
   (a) What did Lincoln do when he could not return the book to the owner?
   (b) Why did the people of the southern states need slaves? How did they treat them?
   (c) What was the main reason for the Civil War in America?
   (d) What did Lincoln do at the end of the Civil War in America?
   (e) How did Lincoln die?

2. **Fill in the blanks.**

(a) Lincoln was born ....; then his family moved to ....

(b) When Lincoln travelled to New Orleans he went down two rivers, the .... and the ....

(c) Abraham Lincoln decided to become a ....

(d) Civil War in America started in ....

(e) The .... won a great victory at Gettysburg.

(f) Lincoln's death in .... was mourned by all people.

3. **Match the following.**

(a) Honest Abe	Lincoln's murderer
(b) John Wilkes Booth	Headed the northern states
(c) General Grant	Lincoln's nickname
(d) General Lee	Lived in Indiana with Lincoln
(e) Dave Jackson	Headed the southern states

Things to do

1. **Find out.**

Find out where the President of America lives, what the house is called and see if you can get a picture of it to stick in your scrapbook.

2. **Want to try a web-based activity about Abraham Lincoln? Check the following website.**

http://www.siec.k12.in.us/~west/proj/lincoln/
(accessed on 12 August 2006)

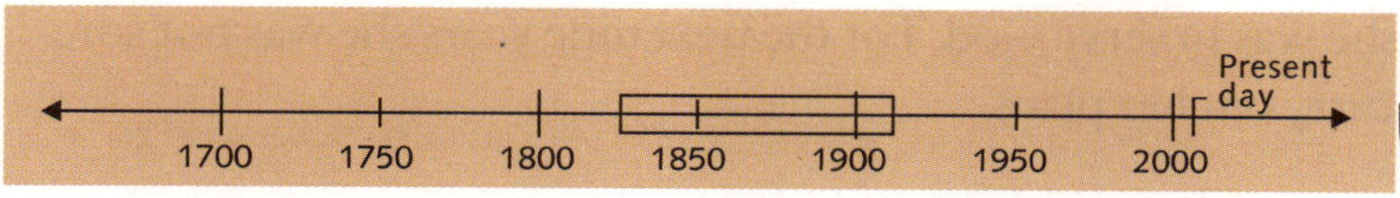

Florence Nightingale

—The lady with the lamp

In 1820, a baby girl was born to a rich British couple who were spending their holiday at a place called Florence in Italy. The baby was named Florence after the name of the city in which she was born. In Britain at that time, Florence was a new name for girls, but in later years, it became popular because of the fame of Florence Nightingale.

In due course, the Nightingales returned to Britain. Florence was taught by her father who did not like to send his daughters to school. Florence and her sister Parthe had to work hard at many subjects like philosophy and mathematics. She learnt many foreign languages too. Florence worked hard, and in addition, helped her mother in a number of ways. She had a habit of writing her private thoughts on pieces of paper. When she was seventeen, she had a **vision**, just as Joan of Arc of France had hundreds of years before her. She wrote:

'On 7 February 1837, God spoke to me and called me to His service.'

However, when Joan of Arc had a vision she received clear instructions as to what she was to do. Florence

Words to remember

vision : a dream or a similar experience, especially of a religious kind.

calm : not excited, nervous or troubled; quiet.

delicate : something showing or needing much skill or careful treatment.

suspicious : doubtful.

committee : a group of people appointed to deal with a particular matter.

only knew that she was to serve God. For the next nine years she was not sure how she would carry out her plans.

Florence grew up into a beautiful young girl. As a daughter of rich parents, she wore beautiful dresses and was often seen at the parties that were given by rich people in London. But she was not happy at these places. She always remembered that she was to serve God and waited for her chance to do so.

Florence Nightingale

In 1842, the crops failed in Britain. The country suffered from what was almost a famine. People in the villages were starving. People in the towns had to work for almost nothing. London was full of people without work, and the hospitals were full too. Florence Nightingale was pained to see the misery of the poor and she began to realize that God's service might mean working for the poor of the world.

She always felt kindly towards the sick and wanted to nurse them. As she read about the miserable conditions in the hospitals, her ambition to become a nurse became stronger. She wanted to improve those places where the sick people were left uncared for, the medicines were lacking, and the people working in these hospitals were not devoted.

Not far from the Nightingales' home was a hospital, and Dr Fowler was the chief doctor there. One night her parents invited him to dinner, and after dinner they all sat talking in the drawing room.

'My dear Mama,' said Florence, 'I have been thinking about my future. I have been thinking about what I want to do in life.'

'And what have you decided, dear Florence?' asked her mother.

Dr Fowler and her father were listening carefully.

'I have decided that I want to be a nurse,' said Florence.

'A nurse!' cried her father. 'How can you be a nurse? That means working in a hospital!'

'Yes, Father, it does. It means learning about nursing too. Could I go to Dr Fowler's hospital and spend some months there in learning how to be a nurse?'

Both her mother and father were extremely angry. When Dr Fowler saw how angry they were, he tried to **calm** them.

'I agree with you,' he said, 'that it would be quite impossible for a **delicate** and beautiful girl like Florence to train as a nurse.'

In those days hospitals were overcrowded and dirty. No respectable woman would ever choose nursing as a career because nurses then had to work under the most unpleasant conditions. No wonder that Florence's parents would not let her go to a hospital, but expected her to live at home and be a fashionable young lady.

At that time, Florence was unable to do anything except obey her parents. But she did not give up her idea. She read as many books about nursing as she could and spent her time looking after sick people in the villages near her home. She visited hospitals whenever she could. Once, when she went to Germany for a holiday, she was allowed to train at a good hospital for three months, where she learnt a great deal. At last her parents allowed her to become superintendent of a small nursing home, where she proved herself to be an excellent organizer.

In 1854, the Crimean War broke out between Britain, France and Turkey on the one side, and Russia on the other. In the Crimean Peninsula, the Russians had a base at a place called Sebastopol, on the Black Sea. The French and British soldiers landed on the northern coast of the Crimea and proceeded southwards in order to attack Sebastopol. They tried to sreach Sebastopol by crossing the river Alma. Unfortunately there were not enough boats to take the equipment as well as the men. The soldiers crossed the river with great courage but they left behind their tents, cooking pots, medicines and hospital equipment. Almost immediately, cholera broke out.

By the time the army surrounded the city, the Russians had strengthened their defences. The British and the French army laid a siege through the long Crimean winter. A fierce battle followed. The poet Tennyson has described it in his famous poem, 'The Charge of the Light Brigade'. He wrote:

Into the Valley of Death

Rode the six hundred.

Only 195 of these came back. The rest lay dead or wounded. The wounded men lay on the ground in the open. There were no beds, no medical supplies, and only a few surgeons. All these cholera patients and also the wounded soldiers were sent to a place called Scutari on the other side of the Black Sea. In Scutari, a large building had been converted into a hospital by the British, but it was not big enough for all the sick and wounded soldiers who arrived in large numbers.

The people of Britain naturally knew nothing of this. A man called Russell was sent out to report on the war by a newspaper called *The Times* in London. He sent his reports home and they included a terrible description of the way in which the British soldiers were being neglected in the hospital. Soon everyone in Britain was talking about it. Russell wrote:

> 'Are there no devoted women among us able and willing to go forth to the hospital of Scutari? Are none of the daughters of England, at this extreme hour of need, ready for such a work of mercy?'

He went on to say that the French hospitals were much better, that they had nurses who were nuns, called the Sisters of Charity, and they nursed the French with care and devotion.

Florence Nightingale knew immediately that this was her life's mission. She wrote to a friend in the government and to her family's surprise, she left immediately for Scutari with forty nurses. She arrived there on 15 November 1854. It was winter and the weather was bitterly cold. Every day more and more wounded soldiers poured into the hospital.

When Florence arrived in Scutari with her team of nurses, she did not receive a very happy welcome from the doctors. They were **suspicious** and uncooperative. Florence, however, patiently brought about a number of changes in the hospital. *The Times* had raised some funds and Florence used this money well. She repaired the hospital, bought blankets and soap, medical supplies of all kinds and improved the food. She organized the work of the doctors and the nurses, and the doctors soon realized that although she looked weak, she was determined.

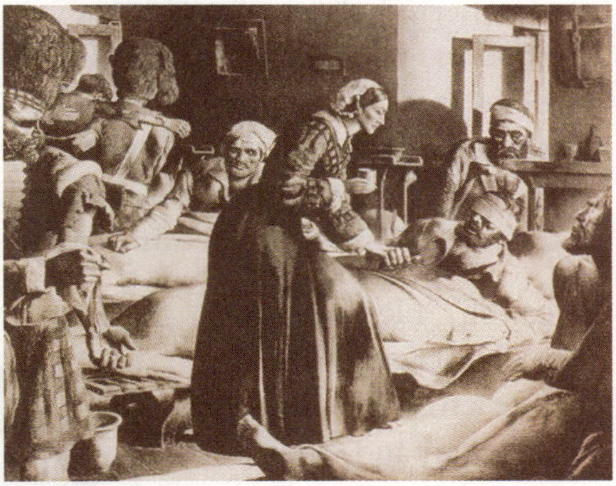

Florence Nightingale at Scutari

Not only did she carry out this great task of organization but she also did a great deal of nursing herself. She worked for long hours in the hospital wards, sometimes spending the entire day and night. Every night, she walked around the whole hospital with a light in her hand. The wounded soldiers called her, 'The Lady with the Lamp', a name by which she is remembered even today.

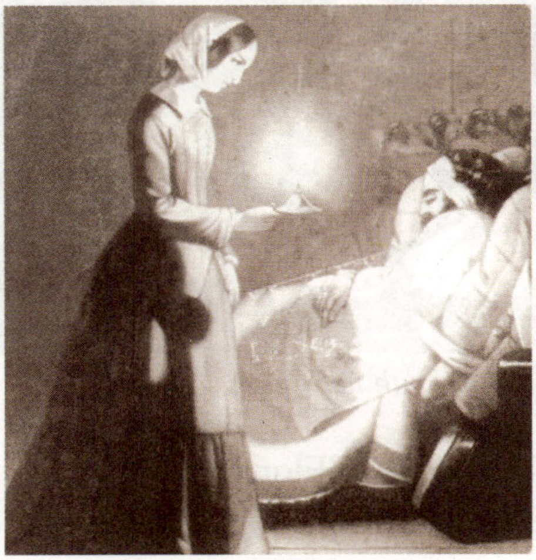

Florence came to be known as 'The Lady with the Lamp'

Florence Nightingale travelled throughout the Crimea working as hard as she could. She often fell ill, but as soon as she was well again, she was off to visit another hospital. The war ended in September 1855. Florence refused to go home until all the patients had left the hospital at Scutari.

When she returned to Britain she was famous, but she did not want people to honour her. Instead, she started criticizing the hospitals in Britain. She wanted them to change the dark, dreary buildings into places where people could get well quickly and happily. The government asked her to serve on a **committee**. She spent all her time in working to change things in hospitals, especially the army hospitals.

Did you know?

The first textbook for nurses was written by Florence Nightingale which is titled *Notes on Nursing* (1860). It has been translated into many languages.

In 1860, the people of Britain wanted to reward her for her services during the war. They collected a large sum of money, £45,000 and presented it to her. With this money, she set up a training school for nurses in London called the Nightingale School for Nurses. These nurses were given proper training and the Nightingale nurses soon became famous all over the country.

Florence with her nurses

Since 1857, Florence had been ill but carried on all her work from her bed. She wrote letters and reports and gave lectures and advised different people on the setting up of hospitals and the training of nurses. All this hard work affected her eyes and she became blind in 1901. Florence was given the Order of Merit in 1907 by King Edward VII—the first woman ever to receive this award. She died in 1910 at a very advanced age of ninety years. The name of Florence Nightingale will always be remembered for the contributions she made in developing the nursing system.

Exercises

1. Answer the following.

(a) What made Florence decide that she would be a nurse?

(b) Write what you know about the Crimean War.

(c) How did the people of Britain come to know about the condition of the sick and wounded soldiers in the Crimean War?

(d) What did Florence Nightingale do to improve the hospital at Scutari?

(e) Why is Florence remembered as 'The Lady with the Lamp'?

(f) What did Florence do with the money she got as a reward?

2. Fill in the blanks.

(a) Florence was born in the year ....

(b) The Russians had a base at a place called .... near the Black Sea.

(c) The poet .... has described the Crimean war in a famous poem.

(d) Florence was given the .... by King Edward VII.

(e) Florence Nightingale died in ....

3. Choose the correct answer.

(a) Florence Nightingale wanted to become a ....

i) Nurse ii) Painter iii) Engineer iv) Dancer

(b) The Crimean War broke out between Britain, France and .... on the one side, and Russia on the other.

i) Venezuela ii) Turkey iii) Sweden iv) Austria

(c) Florence Nightingale's sister's name was ....

i) Joan of Arc ii) Russell iii) Fowler iv) Parthe

(d) Sebastopol in the Crimean Peninsula is located on the............

i) Red Sea ii) Black Sea iii) Arabian Sea

iv) Mediterranean Sea

Things to do

1. **Drawing activity.**

   Try to draw a picture of Florence Nightingale with a lamp.

2. **Make a first aid kit.**

   Try to make a first aid kit with a cardboard box. Paste white paper on it and draw a red cross. Put in some essential things for first aid: Gloves (2 pairs); Tweezers; Needle, First-aid book; Sterile adhesive bandages; Small roll of absorbent gauze or gauze pads of different sizes; Adhesive tape; Triangular and roller bandage; Cotton; Band-aids (Plasters); Scissors; Pen torch; Antiseptic (Savlon or Dettol); Thermometer; Tube of petroleum jelly or any other lubricant; Assorted sizes of safety pins; Cleansing agent/soap.

3. **Try a quiz on Florence Nightingale on the internet. Visit the following site.**

   http://www.bbc.co.uk/schools/famous people/standard/nightingale/indexgarden of praise.com/bdnight (accessed on 12 August 2006)

Laxmibai

—The brave Rani of Jhansi

Born in the holy city of Varanasi on 21 November 1835, Laxmibai had been named Manikarnika after one of the bathing ghats of the city. Her mother called her Manu. Her father was a **courtier** in the court of the Maratha ruler, Peshwa Baji Rao II. Little Manu was a great favourite of the old Peshwa. She was a brave girl and full of life. One day, a large cobra appeared in the court. It raised its hood and frightened everyone. The snake was killed. Manu said, 'But I liked it.'

'You liked the snake, child?' asked the Peshwa.

Laxmibai

Words to remember

courtier : a companion or advisor of a king or queen at court.

horoscope : diagram of positions of planets at the time of a person's birth for the purpose of forecasting future events.

pension : regular payment made by the state to somebody after long service or retirement.

cartridges : tubes or cases containing explosives with bullets.

comrades : loyal friends.

hurled : threw.

rebel : a person who fights against, or refuses to serve the established government.

'No, not the snake,' said Manu. 'But it's wonderful to be able to put fear into everyone, and in such a little time too.'

The Peshwa laughed and asked, 'Would you like to frighten us?'

Manu never dreamt that she would become a queen. Gangadhar Rao, the ruler of Jhansi, a small state in Uttar Pradesh, had just lost his queen. He sent his priest, Tantia Dikshit, in search of a girl from a noble family. Dikshit came to the court of the old Peshwa. In the court he saw Manu. Dikshit was very pleased to see Manu. He told the old Peshwa and Manu's father, 'I like this girl. I think she will be a good queen for my king.'

Dikshit then consulted Manu's **horoscope** and told Manu's father, 'Your daughter will become a queen. Her husband's family will become very famous because of her deeds.'

A portrait of the young Rani possibly at the time of her wedding

And so Manu and Gangadhar Rao, the Maharaja of Jhansi, were married. At the time of her wedding, her husband's people gave her a new name—Laxmibai.

As a queen, Laxmibai spent her time cooking delicious dishes for her husband and looking after the excellent library in the palace. In 1853, Gangadhar Rao became seriously ill, and lay dying. The British East India Company had already declared that once the ruler of an Indian state died without a child, the state would at once come under the rule of the company. To save Jhansi from passing on to the British, a day before his death, the Maharaja adopted a son and called him Damodar Rao.

In 1854, Lord Dalhousie, who was then the Governor-General instructed Major Ellis, his agent in Jhansi, to bring Jhansi under British rule. He refused to accept the six-year old Damodar Rao as the prince. Major Ellis appeared at the Rani's court and read out a long announcement. He declared that the East India

Company would rule Jhansi from then on. The Rani would receive a **pension** and she would be allowed to live in the palace. Even as Major Ellis read on, the Rani's clear, angry voice was heard from behind the curtain, *'Meri Jhansi nahi dungi.'* (I'll never give up my Jhansi.)

Lord Dalhousie

During the next three years, Laxmibai lived quietly in the palace on the small pension she received from the British rulers. The new rulers saw no cause for anxiety. Everything was peaceful in Jhansi.

In May 1857, the Indian soldiers of the company's army revolted against their British masters. They had many complaints. They were paid much less than the British soldiers. They could never rise to the higher posts in the army. They were forced to violate the rules of their religion when they were made to shave off their beards, give up their turbans, or sent to fight wars across the seas. Whenever they protested, they were cruelly punished. In Bengal, thirty soldiers had been blown off from the mouths of guns. Many were shot and hanged at Vellore, Barrackpore and Afghanistan. In 1857, a new rifle was introduced in the army. Its **cartridges** had a greased paper cover. The end of the cover had to be bitten off before the cartridge could be loaded into the rifle. The grease was made of beef and pig fat. Hindus were not supposed to taste beef; Muslims were not permitted to taste pork. At Meerut, ninety soldiers, Hindus and Muslims, refused to use the cartridges. They were dismissed and put in chains. But the rest of the soldiers released their **comrades**, killed their officers, and marched to Delhi. In Delhi, they chose the old Mughal emperor Bahadur Shah as the emperor of India and drove out the British from Delhi. The revolt spread all over northern and central India.

In June, the soldiers of Jhansi rose in revolt. They captured the fort and killed the British officers. In March 1858, the British attacked Jhansi. The Rani herself was in charge of defending the fort. As the men fired the guns, the women worked at repairing the walls hit by enemy shells. When the soldiers in the fort had no ammunition left, they **hurled** stones, logs, and whatever else they could lay their hands on at the enemy. Eventually, the British captured the palace and killed the people within mercilessly. They were avenging the killing of the British officers a year earlier.

The Rani Mahal inside Jhansi Fort

Luckily Laxmibai slipped out of the fort under cover of night, dressed as a man, with her adopted son and a small band of soldiers. The Rani rode on and on, covering 21 miles in one night. In the morning, the British cavalry chased her. While her brave soldiers fought with them and were all slain, the Rani escaped.

A stamp with a picture of Tantia Tope

Laxmibai joined Tantia Tope, the **rebel** leader. They captured Gwalior. The British army rushed towards Gwalior because the ruler of Gwalior was their ally. On 17 June 1858, on their way to Gwalior, they faced the brave Rani leading a small band of soldiers on horseback. The Rani and her soldiers were all dressed

A wall painting showing Rani Laxmibai with her son and Tantia Tope behind her

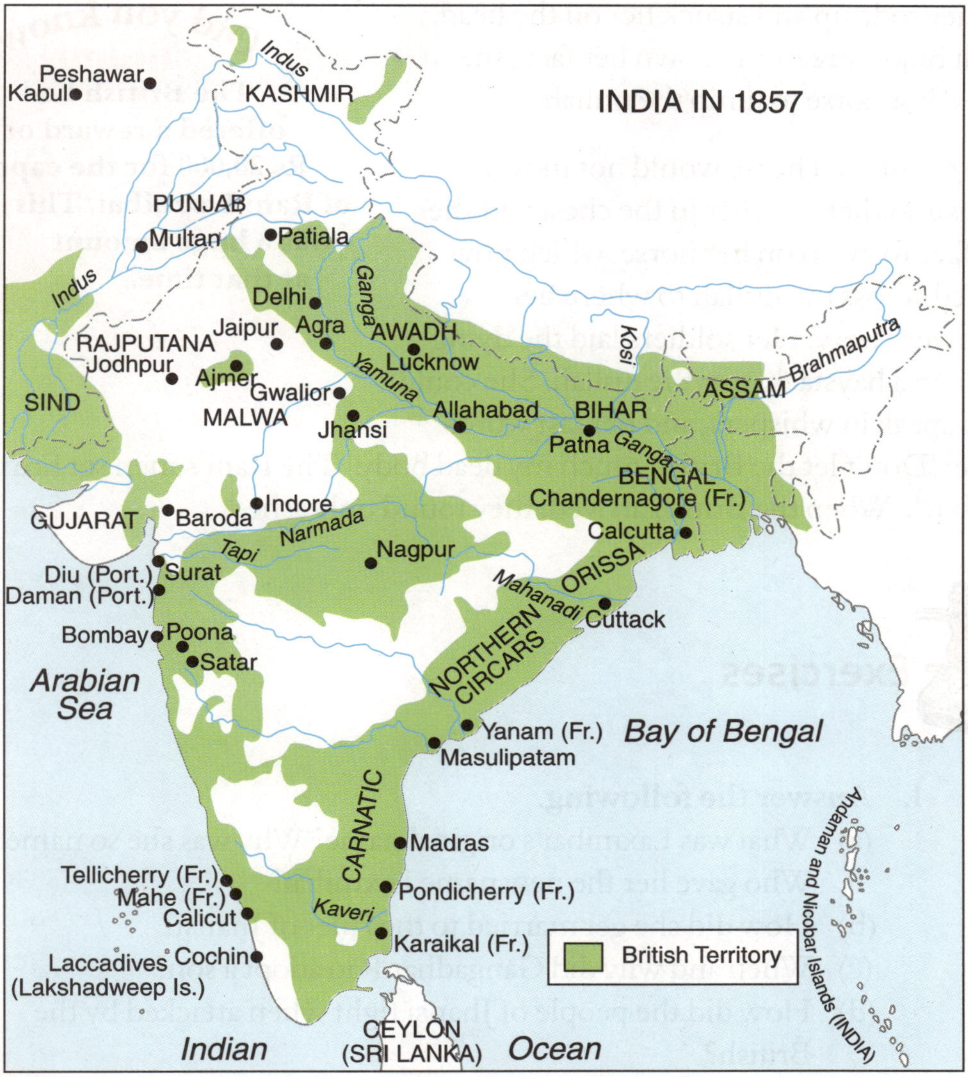

alike in blue uniforms and white turbans. Close to the Rani rode Mandarbai, her lifelong friend and companion, a Muslim girl. Chased by the British soldiers, the Rani urged her horse towards the Sonerakha Nullah, a narrow stream between steep rocks. It was a hot day. The Rani had been fighting for ten hours at a stretch. Still she was as determined as ever. She was about to cross the nullah when she heard a cry from behind. She turned and saw a British soldier killing Mandarbai. She killed the soldier with one stroke of her sword. Another soldier rode up and struck her on the head. With blood streaming down her face, she urged her horse to jump the nullah.

The frightened horse would not move. A British soldier shot her in the chest and she fell face forward on her horse, which now leaped across the nullah to where her followers were. Her soldiers laid the dying Rani on a haystack near the nullah. She could only speak in whispers, and her last words were: 'Don't let the British touch my dead body.' The Rani's men set fire to the haystack. When the British arrived, they found only ashes.

Did you know?

The British had offered a reward of Rs 20,000 for the capture of Rani Laxmibai. This was a huge amount at that time.

Exercises

1. Answer the following.

(a) What was Laxmibai's original name? Why was she so named? Who gave her the new name Laxmibai?

(b) How did she get married to the ruler of Jhansi?

(c) When and why did Gangadhar Rao adopt a son?

(d) How did the people of Jhansi fight when attacked by the British?

(e) Who was Mandarbai? What did the Rani do when she heard her cry?

(f) What was the Rani's last wish? Was it fulfilled?

2. Fill in the blanks.

(a) Laxmibai was born in the year ....

(b) In 1857, the .... of the British East India Company's army revolted against their masters.

(c) At ...., ninety soldiers refused to use the cartridges.
(d) In March 1858, the British attacked ....
(e) Laxmibai joined ...., the rebel leader.

3. **Say whether the following are True or False.**
(a) Manu and Gangadhar Rao were married to each other.
(b) Damodar Rao was the adopted son of Maharaja Gangadhar Rao.
(c) In 1854, Major Ellis was the Governor-General of the British East India Company.
(d) The Indian soldiers were forced by the British to violate the rules of their religion.
(e) Mandarbai was killed by Laxmibai's soldiers.

Things to do

1. **For your scrapbook.**

Collect pictures of forts and stick them in your book. Find out about any one famous fort of India and write ten sentences on it in your scrapbook.

2. **Find out.**

Poems on the life of Rani Laxmibai are very popular. Find one such poem and recite it in your class.

3. **For some interesting information check out the following website.**

http://www.freeindia.org/biographies/jhansi/ (accessed on 12 August 06)

Rabindranath Tagore

—India's first Nobel Prize winner

Rabindranath Tagore was one of the greatest **literary** figures of India. He was a writer, poet, novelist, educator, social reformer, freedom fighter and above all, a great **humanitarian** and philosopher. He was truly a product of both traditional Indian, and modern Western cultures.

Rabindranath Tagore in 1915

Words to remember

literary: occupied with books or literature or written composition.
humanitarian: person who seeks to promote human welfare.
playwright: a person who writes plays
lecture: a talk given to a group of people to inform them or teach them something.
knighted: one who has been given a special honour by British king or queen and has the title Sir before his name.
insight: to see and understand the truth.
funeral: religious ceremony for burying or cremating a dead person.
massacre: killing of a large number of people in a cruel way.

Tagore was born on 7 May 1861 in Calcutta. He was the ninth son of Debendranath and Sarada Devi. His father was a social reformer and a scholar. He was married to Mrinalini Devi in 1883 at the age of twenty-two. They had two sons and three daughters.

Tagore started to compose poems at the age of eight. His first published poem was *Abhilaash.* At seventeen, Tagore's first book, *Kabi Kahini*, a collection of poems, was published by his friend. His songs, popularly known as 'Rabindra Sangeet', are quite a favourite among the Bengalis.

His early life was greatly influenced by religion and arts, mainly literature, music and painting. He grew up on three languages—Sanskrit, Bengali and English. Most of his education was at home, but in 1878, was sent to Britain for formal education. He did not stay there for long.

Rabindranath Tagore at work

He returned to India and pursued a career as a writer, **playwright**, song writer, poet, philosopher and educator. Things changed for him in 1912 when he returned to Britain. During the long sea voyage from India to Britain, he translated his latest selections of Bengali poems, *Gitanjali*, into English. Almost all his work prior to this was written in his mother tongue, Bengali. When Tagore's friend in Britain, Rothenstein, saw the translation, he showed the poems to W.B. Yeats, a leading British poet of the time. Yeats was all praise for the work.

Gitanjali was published in September 1912. Both poetry and Tagore became an instant hit, first in London and then in the entire world. Less than a year later, in 1913, Rabindranath received the Nobel Prize for literature. He was the first Asian to be given this award. He began world tours giving **lectures** on inter-cultural harmony and understanding. In 1915, he was **knighted** by the British King George V and came to be known as Sir Rabindranath Tagore.

Tagore was well educated and quite knowledgeable of the Western culture, especially Western poetry and science. With his translations of some of his poems into English, he became a known figure in the West. He wanted the East and the West to be united, and to merge the ancient and modern knowledge. He became the voice of India's spiritual and cultural heritage to the world.

Rabindranath Tagore wrote over one thousand poems, eight volumes of short stories, almost two dozen plays, eight novels, and many books and essays on philosophy, religion, education and social topics.

In his collection of poetry, some of the popular ones are 'Manasi', 'Sonar Tari', 'Gitanjali', 'Gitimalya' and 'Balaka'. The English translations of his poetry, include 'The Gardener', 'Fruit-Gathering', 'The Fugitive', 'Song Offerings'. Tagore's major plays are *Raja, Dakghar, Achalayatan, Muktadhara,* and *Raktakaravi*. He has also written several volumes of short stories and a number of novels. *Gora, Ghare-Baire*, and *Yogayog* are well known amongst them. As a novelist, Tagore gave a good **insight** into the upper middle-class life in Bengal and the impact of Western ideas on Indian life. Besides these, he wrote musical dramas, dance dramas, essays of all types, travel diaries, and two autobiographies. He wrote two important poems, 'The Sick Bed' and 'The Recovery', towards the end of his life. 'The Ocean of Peace', a song , which he had requested while he was ill, was sung for him at his **funeral**.

Besides writing, his other great love was music in Bengali. He composed music and lyrics of more than two thousand songs. Two of his songs became the national anthems of India and Bangladesh. In 1929, he even began painting. Many of his paintings can be found in museums today.

Veiled Woman by Rabindranath Tagore

In 1901, he founded his school, the Shantiniketan, in West Bengal. The school was a great success and gave birth to Viswabharati which strongly supported the emerging Western and Indian philosophy and education. It became a university in 1921. He gave all his money from Nobel Prize and royalty from his books to this university. In 1940, Oxford University arranged a special ceremony in Shantiniketan to honour the poet with Doctorate of Literature. Most of Tagore's life was spent at Shantiniketan.

Tagore and Mahatma Gandhi

Tagore was a true and devoted nationalist. He was actively involved in the freedom struggle when the agitation against the partition of Bengal in 1905 was at its peak. In 1919, he publicly disowned his knighthood to protest against the Jallianwalla Bagh **massacre** at Amritsar, where the British troops had opened fire at the unarmed Indians. In addition, he wrote many patriotic poems and national songs and attended protest meetings. His song, *Jana Gana Mana* is now sung all over India as the national anthem.

Tagore with Einstein

Rabindranath Tagore and Albert Einstein, the great scientist, met four times between 1930-31. They had both won the Nobel Prize, Tagore for literature in 1913, Einstein for physics in 1921. A relative of Einstein, described Tagore as 'the poet with the head of a thinker' and Einstein as 'the thinker with the head of a poet'. Though they had different nationalities, background and occupations, yet they were connected by their curiosity about the other's contributions, their search for truth and their love of music. Their dialogues were published in the *New York Times* magazine in 1930.

Tagore passed away on 7 August 1941 in Calcutta. He has left behind 28 volumes of prose, poetry, plays and lectures, over 2500 songs and over 2000 paintings and drawings. Today, we need his messages of world peace and love of humanity, perhaps even more, than when Tagore first wrote his words.

Did you know?

He is the only person to have written the national anthems of two countries—*Amar Shonar Bangla* of Bangladesh and *Jana Gana Mana* of India.

Exercises

1. **Answer the following.**
   (a) Who was Rabindranath Tagore?
   (b) How did Tagore become world famous in 1912?
   (c) Why was Tagore known as Sir Rabindranath Tagore? Why did he disown the title Sir in 1919?
   (d) Describe Tagore's role as a patriot.
   (e) Why do you think we need Tagore's poems and songs today?

2. **Fill in the blanks.**
   (a) Tagore's songs, popularly known as '.............', are quite a favourite among the Bengalis.
   (b) .... was published in September 1912.
   (c) In 1901, Tagore founded his school, the .... in West Bengal.
   (d) Tagore's song, '..............' is now sung all over India as the national anthem.
   (e) Tagore passed away on .... 1941 in ....

3. **Say whether the following are True or False.**
   (a) Tagore's first published book was *Abhilaash*.

(b) In 1913, Rabindranath received the Nobel Prize for literature.

(c) Tagore translated his latest selections of English poems, *Gitanjali*, into Bengali.

(d) In 1940, Delhi University arranged a special ceremony in Shantiniketan to honour the poet with Doctorate of Literature.

(e) Two of his songs became the national anthems of India and Bangladesh.

Things to do

1. **Recitation.**
   Learn a poem of Tagore. Then have an elocution day in your class and recite it.

2. **Write a story.**
   Do you want to become a writer like Tagore? Write a story in about 300 words, using your imagination, and share it with your friends.

Unit Test 1

Maximum Marks: 15

1. Give one word for the following. **½×6=3**

(a) A formal meeting for discussion between representatives
(b) Person who seeks to promote human welfare
(c) A series of rulers all belonging to the same family
(d) A system of government in which the representatives are elected
(e) A group of people appointed to deal with a particular matter
(f) Soldiers fighting on horses, elephants or armoured vehicles

2. Answer the following. **1×6=6**

(a) What was the Boston Tea Party?
(b) Why were some writers unfair to Tipu Sultan?
(c) What was the result of Napoleon's campaign in Russia?
(d) What kind of government did Simon Bolivar want to give his country?
(e) Mention Garibaldi's only ambition. When did it become a reality?
(f) When did the Crimean War begin? What did Russell write in his report?

3. Fill in the blanks. **½×8=4**

(a) ...., the Governor-General, wanted to crush the power of Tipu Sultan.
(b) Napoleon was finally defeated at .... in the year 1815.
(c) .... is known as the 'George Washington of South America'.
(d) .... gave up his title to protest against the Jallianwala Bagh massacre.
(e) Abraham Lincoln is chiefly remembered for getting rid of..........
(f) .... is known as the tiger of Mysore.
(g) Lord .... instructed his agent Major Ellis to bring .... under British rule.

4. On an outline map of the world mark the following. **½×4=2**

(a) USA (b) Bolivia (c) Italy (d) France

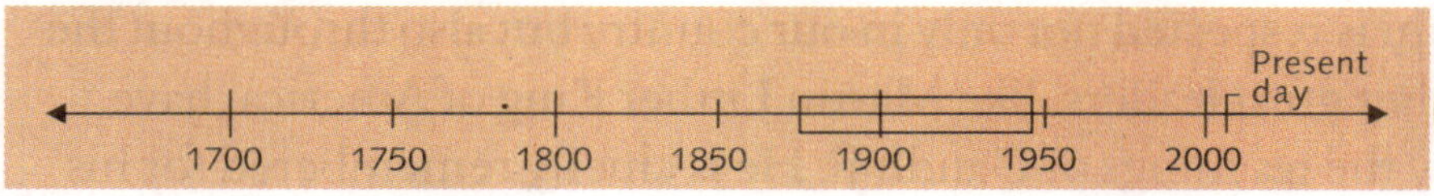

Mahatma Gandhi

—The father of the nation

You have read in Chapters 2 and 7 about the spread of British rule in India. After almost 200 years of British rule, in 1947, India won its independence. Mahatma Gandhi, popularly called the 'Father of the Nation', played a very important part in the Indian struggle for independence against Britain. He was one of the greatest leaders India has ever had. He tried to win freedom for our country, not through bloodshed but through non-violence, that is, without the use of force. This was his greatest achievement.

Mahatma Gandhi

Words to remember

deceiving : cheating.
ashram : a place of retirement for religious meditation.
untouchables : people who could not be touched and were looked down upon.
bonfires : large fires made outdoors for burning rubbish or as a part of celebration.
imposed : laid, charged.
fast : to eat little or no food for a period of time.
riots : disorder; disturbances.
immemorial : for a very long time; beyond the reach of memory.

Mahatma Gandhi is respected not only in our country but also throughout the world. Many other great leaders, like Martin Luther King of America, have been inspired by the teachings of Gandhiji. He is chiefly remembered for his peace-loving outlook that guided all his actions.

Mohandas Karamchand Gandhi was born on 2 October 1869 in a town called Porbandar in Gujarat. His father was a government official. Gandhi's mother was a very religious Hindu lady. Gandhi was greatly influenced by her. Young Gandhi passed his childhood in Porbandar. When he was seven, his father left Porbandar for Rajkot, another place in Gujarat. Mohandas joined a primary school. He was a shy child and avoided all company. He spent his time in reading books. At the age of thirteen, a year after he reached high school, he was married to a young girl named Kasturba.

From his early childhood, Gandhi always tried to speak the truth. He hated **deceiving** anybody. He loved to read the story of Raja Harishchandra, who was extremely virtuous and truthful. God wanted to test Harishchandra and so put him through a great deal of hardship but the good Raja never strayed from the path of truth. 'Why shouldn't we all be truthful like Harishchandra?' asked Gandhi, and he thought about it day and night. Truth was an ideal he followed all his life.

In his early teens, Gandhi made a friend who proved to be a bad influence on him. Mohandas was brought up in a strict vegetarian family where eating meat was strictly forbidden. He also took to smoking and sometimes stole money in order to buy cigarettes. But soon he realized how sad his parents would be if they came to know about his wrong deeds. The more he thought about it the sadder he became. At last one day he decided to confess to his father. Mohandas wrote a letter to him telling him of his misdeeds and also promising never to steal again. He could not bear to tell this to his father himself.

The next day Mohandas went with the letter to his father's room. His father took the letter.

'What is this?' he asked.

'A letter, Father. Please read it,' said Mohandas with his head bowed in shame.

His father opened the letter and read it slowly. Then he closed his eyes and sat quietly, while tears rolled down his cheeks. He was sad and hurt but did not show any anger. Mohandas felt ashamed but he was also grateful to his father for not scolding him. He realized that his confession had pleased his father. This incident taught him the value of ahimsa, i.e., the ability to deal with matters gently without showing any violence. Gandhiji in his later life always preached ahimsa or non-violence.

Soon after this, at the age of eighteen, Mohandas was sent to a college. After a year, his family decided to send him to Britain to study law and become a lawyer. He sailed from Bombay in 1888. In Britain, he devoted much time to his studies but he also found time to read other books. He was especially interested in religious books and read a great deal about Hinduism, Christianity and Islam. In 1891, Gandhiji became a lawyer and returned to India. He set up his own office at Rajkot and started working as a lawyer. A couple of years later, he received an offer to go to South Africa to fight a case for a big company. Gandhiji wanted a change and so he accepted the offer.

In South Africa, soon after reaching the port of Durban, he realized that people with dark skins were not welcome in the country. The white men who ruled the land looked down upon dark-skinned people and treated them very badly indeed. The Africans and the Indians were kept at a distance from the whites everywhere. Dark-skinned people were made to live in special parts of the towns and many laws against them were cruel and unjust.

Mahatma Gandhi with his colleagues in South Africa

Once, for example, soon after he arrived, Gandhiji set off on a train to do some business for a rich man who had employed him. He went to the station and bought a first-class ticket. He walked slowly up the platform and at last found an empty compartment. He went inside, sat down and started reading a book. After a few minutes a white man appeared at the door.

'Who are you?' he shouted at Gandhi.

Gandhi looked up and replied politely. 'I am Mohandas Karamchand Gandhi.'

'Get out!' shouted the man. 'You can't travel in a first-class compartment.'

Saying this the man called the guard and together they hurled Gandhi out of the train.

Gandhi soon learnt that this was the usual treatment that the Africans and Indians received from the whites in Africa. He was very hurt to see such an injustice. Although the work for which he had come to South Africa was finished, he decided to stay on and fight for the rights of his countrymen there. After three years, he came back to India to take his wife and children back with him. During his short stay in India, he wrote and told people about the sad condition of the Indians in South Africa. This made him very unpopular with the whites in South Africa when he returned there. But it did not bother him. He continued his noble work and came back to India in 1914 just before the First World War.

Gandhiji and Kasturba on their return to India in 1915

For the next few years, Gandhiji gave all his time and energy to an **ashram** that he founded in Gujarat. Everybody was welcome to join the ashram provided they were prepared to lead a simple life and work with their hands. Gandhiji wanted people to support themselves by working in their own houses. He encouraged them to spin their own cloth on a charkha.

Mahatma Gandhi on the charkha

People from the lower classes were also admitted into this ashram. Gandhiji tried to improve the condition of the lower castes, who were considered to be **untouchables** by the higher classes. He called these neglected people 'Harijans', which means 'the children of God'. He lived with them and ate with them. Harijans were not allowed to visit temples and Gandhiji tried to put a stop to this evil custom. He said that God had made all men equal and so there should be no such difference. Although Gandhiji respected his own religion, Hinduism, he did not look down on other religions. In fact, he preached the equality of all religions.

The British had been ruling over India for almost two centuries. Towards the end of the nineteenth century, the Indians began their struggle for independence. They wanted to rule their own country. The British government made a lot of promises but did not keep them. The Indian freedom fighters were getting restless and wanted to fight openly with the British. At this stage in 1919, Gandhiji came on the scene. He wanted to stop Indians from becoming violent. He believed that India should win freedom from the British through love and non-violence. Gandhiji was already regarded as a leader for all the work he did in South Africa and also in his ashram.

The Gandhi Ashram at Ahmedabad

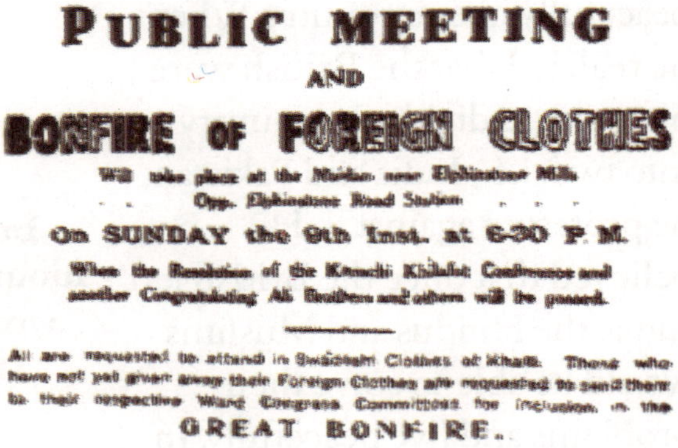

A poster requesting people to wear hand woven cloth and burn all foreign goods

Gandhiji taught the people to oppose the British through non-violence. He started the Non-Cooperation Movement in 1920, when he asked Indians not to cooperate with the British and use only goods made in India. **Bonfires** were lit and British-made clothes were burnt. The British government put Gandhiji and many other people in jail. In 1930, Gandhiji and seventy-eight of his chosen followers went on the famous Dandi March. It was a protest against a tax that the British had **imposed** on salt. Gandhiji's Dandi March inspired people in many other parts of India to rise against the British. Once again, Gandhiji and thousands of people were thrown into prison.

A photograph showing Gandhiji and his followers during the Dandi March

Whenever Gandhiji wanted to protest against anything, he went on a **fast**. Thus, he avoided violent methods. Gandhiji visited many parts of India and gave hope to the people. He spoke to them in plain and simple language and they listened to him in silence and with respect. All Indians began to call him 'Bapu'.

The struggle with the British government was a long and difficult one. Gandhiji wanted Hindus and Muslims to live together peacefully in one country. When he realized that the British were planning to divide the country into two, i.e., India and Pakistan, he protested against it. He believed that once the British left India, the Hindus and Muslims would be able to solve their problems and live peacefully. In 1942, the Quit India Movement was started under the leadership

Did you know?

On the day of the transfer of power to India, Gandhi did not celebrate independence with the rest of India. He was alone in Calcutta mourning the partition of India and working to end the violence that had erupted between the Hindus and the Muslims.

of Gandhiji. The British were asked to leave or quit India. Gandhiji was arrested and put in jail. He began a fast that continued for three weeks. He was then seventy-three years old.

Finally, on 15 August 1947, India became independent; but the country was divided into India and Pakistan. Just before this, fierce **riots** broke out between the Hindus and Muslims. Thousands of people were killed. Gandhiji tried to stop this senseless killing and held many prayer meetings.

On 30 January 1948, while Bapu was on his way to a prayer meeting, a man called Nathuram Godse came out of the crowd and shot Gandhiji dead. What a sad day this was for India and her people! The whole nation wept for this great man.

On his death, Pandit Jawaharlal Nehru said, 'The light has gone out of our lives, and everywhere it is dark. The Father of the Nation is no more. The best prayer we can offer is to give ourselves to Truth and carry on the noble work for which he lived and for which he died... He lives in the hearts of millions and he will live for **immemorial** ages.'

Exercises

1. **Answer the following.**
   (a) What did Gandhiji notice in South Africa regarding the condition of the dark-skinned people?
   (b) How did Gandhiji feel about the untouchables? What did he do to help them?
   (c) Write five sentences about Gandhiji, saying what his ideas were about fighting for the independence of the country.
   (d) Why did Gandhiji start the Quit India Movement?
   (e) When and how did Gandhiji die?

2. **Fill in the blanks.**
   (a) .... was an ideal that Gandhiji followed all his life.
   (b) Gandhiji was married to a young girl named ....
   (c) Gandhiji set up his office at .... and started working as a lawyer.
   (d) In 1930, Gandhiji and his followers began the famous ....
   (e) Gandhiji began the Non-Cooperation Movement in ....

3. **Give one word answers.**
   (a) The year in which India became independent
   (b) The king who inspired Gandhiji to be truthful in life
   (c) The march organized to protest against the salt tax imposed by the British
   (d) The name Indians gave to Gandhiji
   (e) The town where Gandhiji was born

Things to do

1. **Find out.**
   Do you know the place where Gandhiji was cremated? What is it called?

2. **Activity time.**
   Draw a *charkha* in your book.

3. **Check out the following websites.**
   http://www.mkgandhi.com (accessed on 12 August 06)
   http://www.quotationspage.com/quotes/mahatma_gandhi/
   (accessed on 12 August 2006)

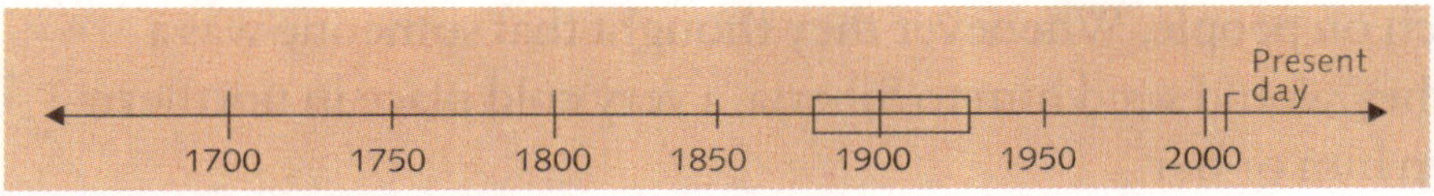

Lenin
—The Russian Bolshevik leader

Towards the close of the nineteenth century, Russia was a large country. It stretched from the Baltic Sea to the Pacific Ocean, a distance of 6,000 miles. This vast land was ruled by one man, the Russian emperor, who was called the Tsar ('Tsar' comes from the Latin word Caesar). He could do anything he liked. He had all the power, and people had to obey him. His word was law. A band of officials, all appointed by the Tsar himself, collected the taxes, and ran the army and the navy. They all belonged to a few rich families, and knew little about how the common people lived.

Most of the Russians were peasants. The peasants paid heavy taxes and lived in poverty. Some of them came to the towns to work in factories. The factory workers lived in crowded **slums** and worked long hours for low **wages** in bad conditions. The peasants, workers and students started to hold protest meetings all over the country. There were many strikes and riots. Tsar Alexander II was killed by a revolutionary in 1881. His son, Alexander III, and grandson, Nicholas II, took stern measures to hold the people in check. The Tsar's

Words to remember

slums : streets of dirty, crowded houses.
wages : payments made or received for work.
exploited : used selfishly, or for one's own profit.
pamphlets : small single pages, usually containing information on a specific subject or expressing political or religious opinions.

police kept watch on people. Whenever they thought that someone was a revolutionary, they would send him to Siberia, a very cold place in northern Russia, and keep him or her imprisoned there.

A painting depicting the day which came to be known as 'Bloody Sunday'

On 22 January 1905, a huge procession of workers marched towards Tsar Nicholas II's palace. They carried the Tsar's portraits and only wanted to beg the Tsar for help. But the police fired on the peaceful people and killed 500 of them. That day came to be known in Russian history as 'Bloody Sunday'. The revolutionary groups began to come together, and soon they found their leader in Lenin.

Lenin as a young boy

Vladimir Ilyich Ulyanov, for that was Lenin's real name, was born on 22 April 1870, in the town of Simbirsk on the river Volga. His father was a teacher of physics and mathematics, and later on, an inspector of schools.

The reddish, bulky, lively Vladimir was the noisiest and the most mischievous of his six children. They called him Kubyshkin— the pot with a fat belly. One of his favourite games was to set traps for birds. But he gave up the game when one of his own birds died in its cage. In the Red Indians' game, he was always the Red Indian. The white men chased him and he hunted wild beasts. At school, Vladimir did extremely well. He was attentive and quiet during lessons, but became wild after the class was over. Vladimir was very fond of his elder brother, Alexander, who was four years older. They both liked to be left alone so that they could concentrate on their studies. Alexander was busy all the time with his microscope, studying insects. Vladimir sat in the same room at his table reading books in Latin.

After passing his final examinations with top marks and a gold medal, Alexander left home to enter the university at St Petersburg. In a letter to his sister a few months later, he wrote, 'I am in good health. I am living as before. I work in the laboratory until six o'clock. The evenings I spend mostly at home.' He was a lonely boy. The other boys teased him as a dreamer. But he soon came to take a great interest in politics. He did not like the way the Tsar's police arrested students on suspicion, and seized their letters in the mail. In 1887, some students formed a group and planned to kill the Tsar. Alexander joined the group. He was asked to prepare a statement for the people and make the bombs. But a few days before the date they had set for killing the Tsar, they were all arrested. Alexander faced the trial bravely. He took the responsibility entirely upon himself to save his comrades. He was sentenced to death and hanged on 8 May. On that very day, Vladimir sat for his mathematics paper in the school-leaving examination. A classmate wrote later, 'We were all terribly agitated. Only Vladimir Ulyanov, seated behind his desk, wrote calmly and unhurriedly. We had six hours for doing our papers. Vladimir finished his work earlier than the rest of us. He was the first to leave the examination hall.' Vladimir stood first in the examination, and won a gold medal.

In the next few months and years, Vladimir thought deeply about his brother's fate. He had heard about revolutionaries in the past. But he had always thought that Alexander couldn't be a revolutionary. A revolutionary couldn't give so much time to the study of worms. Now Vladimir wanted to know why Alexander had given away his life. From the writings of the great poets and novelists, he now turned to history and politics. He read about the revolutions in America and France. He felt that Russia needed a revolution too. He wanted to be a revolutionary himself.

In 1887, Vladimir went to study at the University of Kazan. At Kazan, he learnt about the ideas of the great German thinker, Karl Marx. Marx had tried to show

how the working people did not get what they deserved from their work. The men who owned the land, the mills and factories **exploited** them. He asked his followers to explain to the people how they were exploited. He was confident that once they realized it, the working people would come to own the land, the mills, the factories, and all the machines. They would distribute all the things made and produced to each according to one's needs. Vladimir was inspired by these ideas. In 1895, he visited Marxist thinkers in Switzerland. He returned to Russia convinced that the ideas of Marx should be spread widely.

Karl Marx

Vladimir settled in the city of St Petersburg as a lawyer. Vladimir and his comrades went to the factory workers, found out for themselves how they lived, and taught them how they could improve their life. They wrote **pamphlets** for the workers and distributed them in the factories. Vladimir wrote many pamphlets himself. The police soon arrested him.

Vladimir was sent to Siberia. It was so far away from St Petersburg that the prisoners in Siberia were not kept shut in. Vladimir lived in a small house. Krupskaya, a revolutionary who later became his wife, stayed in the same house. They read books together and talked about the sufferings of the Russian workers. In the evenings they went out for long walks. Vladimir was a good hunter, and there were hares in the woods. One day Vladimir stood before a wood waiting for a hare to come out. His comrades made a loud sound on drums and tins to frighten the hare and make it come out. A fox came straight towards Vladimir. It stopped and looked at him, then slipped away into the woods. Krupskaya rushed up to him. 'Why didn't you shoot?' she asked him. 'This fox was so beautiful,' he said.

Lenin

While in Siberia, Vladimir planned to publish a weekly journal to spread the ideas of Marx and call on the people to start the revolution. When he was released from Siberia, Lenin moved to Germany. The first number of *Iskra* (*The Spark*), Lenin's journal, came out on 1 December 1900 from Stuttgart in Germany. Vladimir used a new signature—Lenin—for the articles he wrote for *Iskra*. One by one he gave up all his hobbies— skating, playing chess, reading Latin poetry, listening to music. All his time was devoted to preparing for the revolution.

The year 1917 began with strikes and large demonstrations against the Tsar. The police were attacked. Even the soldiers joined the demonstrators. In March, the Tsar gave up. Russia came to be ruled by an elected government. Lenin returned to Russia on 16 April 1917. The new government changed nothing. The anger of the people grew. The Bolshevik Party, under Lenin's leadership organized a worker's army and secured arms. Lenin spoke at numerous meetings. The new Bolshevik daily newspaper, *Pravda* (*The Truth*), carried Lenin's appeals to the Russian army. There were clashes between the peasants and the police at many places. The soldiers joined the Bolsheviks and disobeyed the government.

On the morning of 7 November 1917, the Bolsheviks occupied the post offices, telegraph stations, banks and railway stations. There was little struggle, for the people working there were already with the Bolsheviks. In the evening, the Bolshevik soldiers surrounded the Winter Palace in

A photograph showing people marching to the Winter Palace

St Petersburg. The government ministers were inside it. There was fierce fighting between the government troops and the Bolshevik Red Guards. The battle began at 9.45 pm with the guns of the ship *Aurora* firing a loud blank shot in the air. That was the signal for the Red Guards to attack. The battle began to die down in the early hours of the morning. The Winter Palace belonged to the revolutionaries in the morning. A new government led by Lenin took over the next day.

Did you know?

The October Revolution actually started on the night of 6–7 November with the occupation of St Petersburg by groups of Bolsheviks. It is known as the October Revolution because the Russian calendar was a few weeks behind the calendar which most of the world uses.

The new Bolshevik government had to fight against many enemies over the next few years. On 30 August 1918, a young woman tried to shoot Lenin. With two bullets inside him, Lenin's life was in danger. But he became well again and worked hard to give his people peace, food and happiness. Lenin promised a young woman in 1920, 'Your children will never be able to imagine that there was once a time when one man could own houses, factories and riches when thousands of workers went hungry and had no home of their own.'

In 1922, the old Russian empire was transformed into the Union of Soviet Socialist Republics (USSR). It lasted till 1991.

Lenin died in 1924. His body has been preserved. It lies in a tomb in the Red Square in Moscow.

The Red Square

Exercises

1. **Answer the following.**
   (a) What happened on 'Bloody Sunday'?
   (b) Why was Alexander hanged? Why did Vladimir think that Alexander could not be a revolutionary?
   (c) What were Marx's ideas?
   (d) How did Vladimir spend his time in Siberia?
   (e) When did Vladimir take up the new name 'Lenin'?
   (f) What were Lenin's hobbies?
   (g) How did the revolutionaries capture the Winter Palace?

2. **Fill in the blanks.**
   (a) Vladimir was born on .... in the town of ....
   (b) ...., a revolutionary, became his wife.
   (c) The first edition of ...., Lenin's journal, came out in ....
   (d) The new Bolshevik daily newspaper was called ....
   (e) Lenin's body has been preserved in a tomb in the .... in ....

3. **Match the following.**

(a) *Iskra*	*The Truth*
(b) Winter Palace	Great German thinker
(c) *Pravda*	Lenin's brother
(d) Alexander	*The Spark*
(e) Karl Marx	St Petersburg

Things to do

1. **Find Out.**
   Can you draw the flag of Russia? Find out about it from your teacher.

2. **Solve the crossword below.**

   Down

   1. Revolutionaries were sent here
   3. The name of Lenin's party
   5. The Bolshevik newspaper

   Across

   2. The name given to Vladimir
   4. The name given to the Russian Emperor
   6. Journal brought out by Lenin
   7. His ideas inspired Lenin

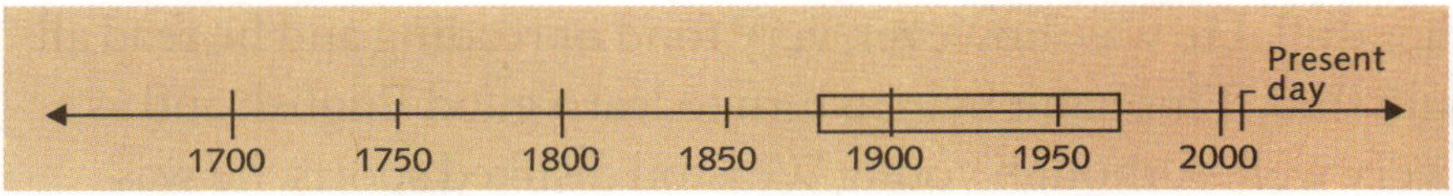

11

Sir Winston Churchill

—The great statesman

Sir Winston Churchill, one of the greatest Englishmen of the twentieth century, was born in 1874. He belonged to a famous family. He was the son of Lord Randolph Churchill, a British politician. The Duke of Marlborough, a great general who lived 200 years earlier, was his ancestor. When Winston was twelve years old, he was sent to an expensive school called Harrow, which he disliked very much. The headmaster was a strict man and used to beat the boys very severely. Churchill was not very fond of his studies. At that time in Britain, the most important subjects in school were Latin and Greek. People thought that it was essential to know Latin and Greek well; but young Winston did not find these subjects interesting. That is why school life to

Sir Winston Churchill

Words to remember

landing grounds : area of land for aircraft to take off from and land on.

equipment : things needed for a specific purpose.

knighthood : the rank, title or state of a knight. (Knight is a man with a rank of honour given by the king or queen for his services to the country, having the title 'Sir' before his name.)

him seemed rather dull. He was, however, very fond of reading and he read all the books he could find. This habit helped him to learn good English and as a result, he wrote very well. Although young Winston disliked sports, he was good at fencing, that is, fighting with long thin swords.

Winston Churchill as a cadet at Sandhurst

When he left school he decided to join the army. He was very proud of his great ancestor, the Duke of Marlborough, and perhaps hoped to be a great general like him. He went to a famous military training college called Sandhurst. When he had finished his training at Sandhurst, he joined a cavalry regiment in 1895 and spent a few months in Cuba during the time of the Cuban War of Independence against Spain. While in Cuba, he wrote about the war and sent reports to an English newspaper. In 1896, his regiment went to India. He lived in Bangalore for some time. Churchill was very brave and adventurous and he wanted to see some real fighting. When he heard that fighting had broken out between the British and the tribesmen of the North-West Frontier Province of India, he marched with the British forces. Every few days he sent back reports of the war to an English newspaper. His reports were read with great interest in Britain. After India, Winston Churchill fought a war in Sudan, a part of Africa which was under the rule of Britain. Here again, Churchill acted as a soldier as well as a reporter.

In 1899, Churchill left the army. He had seen enough of the army life and now he wanted to make his career as a reporter. He also realized that he could earn more money through writing than by being an army officer.

Towards the end of the nineteenth century, the British were engaged in a war with the Boers in South Africa. The Boers were descendants of the people from Holland who had settled down in South Africa in the seventeenth century. Churchill immediately left Britain for Cape Town in South Africa. He was soon sent out with an armed train. Suddenly, the Boers attacked the train and managed to force part of it off the line. Churchill acted bravely. Although the Boers were attacking, he managed to get enough men to make the train start moving again. As the train began to move off along the track, Churchill jumped off the train on to a grassy bank. Suddenly he looked up and saw a man pointing a rifle at him; Churchill was helpless and had to surrender to the Boers. He was immediately taken off to prison, where he was kept with other prisoners to wait for the end of the war.

Churchill as a reporter in South Africa

In prison, Churchill spent all his time planning to escape. At last, one night, when the guards were walking away from the room in which he was imprisoned, he managed to climb out and jump over the wall. Churchill knew he had many miles to go before he could be safe. He also knew that everybody would be looking for him. He walked along until he came to a railway line. At last a train came. It was a goods train and it was going quite slowly; Churchill was able to climb on to it. Early in the morning, before sunrise, he jumped off. He slept during the day, hiding in the woods, and again at night, he climbed on to another train. In this way he travelled for many miles. One night, he came to a mine which was run by a Britisher, who helped him to hide in a dark cave at the bottom of the mine. Churchill had to stay underground in a small hole for a number of days. After many days of adventure, Churchill at last managed to escape from South Africa. When he returned to Britain, he was greeted as a popular hero.

He then decided to begin his career as a politician. In 1900, when he was only twenty-six, he became a Member of Parliament. In the next thirty years, his name became famous in the British Houses of Parliament. He held many important posts in the government at the time of the First World War and played an important part in organizing the naval war staff. In this war, which ended in 1918, Germany was defeated by Britain, France and America, and she became a very weak country.

After the First World War, Churchill returned to politics. Churchill was never afraid of being unpopular and he always boldly said what he thought to be true. He warned the world that Germany was turning slowly into a powerful country and that she was preparing for war again. But nobody wanted to listen.

It was true that in 1933, Germany, under a man named Adolf Hitler, was no longer a weak country. Hitler was an ambitious man and he became very powerful as the leader of a party called the Nazi (National Socialist) Party. By 1934, Hitler was popularly called the 'Führer' in Germany, which means 'the leader of the country'. He promised the Germans that he would make Germany the strongest and the most powerful country in Europe as it had been before the First World War. In 1938–39, he occupied the countries of Austria, Czechoslovakia and Poland and united them with Germany, which became a big empire. Hitler and his Nazis now planned to conquer more land in Europe.

Adolf Hitler

This is what Churchill had feared, but unfortunately the world had not listened to him. In 1939, when Poland was invaded by the German soldiers, Britain and France became frightened of Hitler's growing power and wanted to stop him. In September 1939, Britain and France declared war on Germany and the Second World War broke out. German armies soon occupied many countries in Europe—Norway, Denmark, Belgium and the Netherlands. When Britain had fought on the side of France for nearly a year, the British people realized that they needed a strong man like Churchill as their leader. Churchill was, thus, made the Prime Minister of Britain in May 1940.

In June 1940, Hitler conquered France. Soon the Nazis marched across France and reached the coast in the north of France. They only had to cross the English Channel in order to reach Britain. Before crossing over, Hitler decided to bomb Britain and make her weak. The German planes bombed Britain every night, especially London.

Those were dark days for the people of Britain. At a time when they had to fight the Germans all alone, it was Churchill who helped his countrymen by giving them hope and courage. His speeches at that time are remembered even today. Soon after he became the Prime Minister, he brought courage in the hearts of the British people with these words:

The bombing caused tremendous destruction

> 'We shall defend our island. Whatever the cost may be, we shall fight on the beaches, we shall fight on the fields, and in the streets, we shall fight in the hills; we shall never surrender.'

He did not want his countrymen to be frightened of Nazi Germany. He told them that the aim of the people of Britain was 'Victory at all costs, victory in spite of all terror; however long and hard the road may be'. Whenever he met people he would lift his fingers to make his famous 'V' sign (meaning 'V' for victory). During this time Churchill devoted all his energy in serving his country. He woke up early to write letters. He went to the Houses of Parliament in the afternoon. Later in the day, he visited the soldiers, encouraged them with cheerful words, and looked at the new guns and other war **equipment**. Then he would return to his study and usually work there till three o'clock in the morning. It was Churchill's deep devotion that really helped Britain to stand strong against the mighty power of Germany.

The famous 'V' sign

In June 1941, Germany attacked Russia, and later that year Japan, a friend of Germany, attacked America. As a result, Russia and America were brought into the war and Britain no longer had to fight alone. The war spread to almost all parts of the world. On one side were Germany, Italy and Japan and they were called the Axis Powers. On the other side were the Allied powers—Britain, France, Russia and the USA. In 1944, the Allies crossed the English Channel and landed in Normandy, on the north-west coast of France. Slowly the Germans were driven away from all the countries they had conquered in Europe. The Allies then invaded Germany and in May 1945, Hitler killed himself for fear of being captured by the Allies. With his death, the war came to an end. What a happy day it was for Britain when Churchill announced over the radio that the war with Germany was over!

After the war Churchill did not continue as Prime Minister. He was succeeded by a man named Attlee. Though he was not the Prime Minister, yet Churchill continued to take interest in the politics of his country and the world. He was such an experienced man that the government often sought his advice on political matters. In 1951, at the age of 77, he was elected again as the Prime Minister of Britain. He remained in office till 1955. In 1953, the new Queen of England, Elizabeth II, honoured him with a **knighthood** and he came to be known as Sir Winston Churchill. In the same year, Churchill received the Nobel Prize for literature for his excellent writing. In 1965, the whole world was shaken by the news of his death, at the age of ninety-one. Winston Churchill will always be affectionately remembered by the British people as the Grand Old Man of Britain.

Did you know?

Churchill loved to paint. He created over 500 works during his lifetime and was made an honorary member of the Royal Academy of Arts in London.

Exercises

1. **Answer the following.**
   (a) Write what you know about Churchill's family and ancestors.
   (b) Was Churchill a brave man? Give some examples to illustrate your answer.
   (c) Who was Hitler? What promise did he make to the German people?
   (d) What was Churchill's daily routine during the Second World War?
   (e) When did the war between France, Britain and Germany become a world war? Which countries took part in the Second World War?
   (f) Why was the year 1953 important in the life of Winston Churchill?

2. **Fill in the blanks.**
   (a) Churchill went to a military training college called ....
   (b) In 1899, Churchill left the ....
   (c) At the age of ...., Churchill became a Member of Parliament.
   (d) The First World War ended in the year......................
   (e) The Second World War began in the year ....

3. **Choose the correct answer.**
   (a) Winston Churchill received the Nobel Prize for ....
   i) Science   ii) Medicine
   iii) Peace   iv) Literature

(b) Winston Churchill will always be affectionately remembered by the British people as the ……………….. .

   i) Father of the Nation   ii) Grand Old Man of Britain
   iii) Saviour   iv) Dictator

(c) In 1939, Poland was invaded by the …………… soldiers.

   i) British   ii) Russian
   iii) American   iv) German

(d) In June 1941, Germany attacked …………… .

   i) Russia   ii) France
   iii) Britain   iv) Italy

(e) Winston Churchill died at the age of ……………….. .

   i) ninety-five   ii) ninety
   iii) ninety-one   iv) ninety-six

Things to do

1. **Find out.**
   Do you know of any war that our country has fought during the last ten years? Ask your teacher to help you.

2. **For your scrapbook.**
   Try and find out about any other person who has received a Nobel Prize for literature. Write eight–ten lines about him or her in your scrapbook.

3. **Want to know what life was like for children during the Second World War? Check the following website.**
   http://www.bbc.co.uk/history/ww2children/ (accessed on 12 August 06)

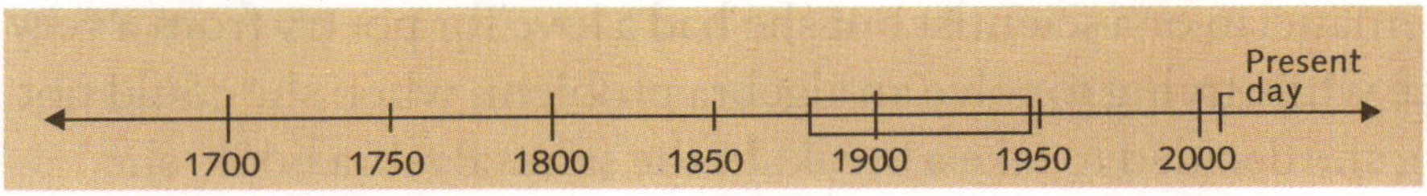

Sarojini Naidu

—The nightingale of India

Rightfully known as the *Bhartiya Kokila*, Sarojini Devi was a great poet, a well-known freedom fighter and a famous **orator**. She was born on 13 February 1879 in Hyderabad in Andhra Pradesh. She belonged to a family of **intellectuals**. Her father was a scientist and philosopher and had founded the Nizam College of Hyderabad, and her mother was a Bengali poet.

Sarojini was a very bright and intelligent child. At the age of twelve, she topped her Matriculation exams in the Madras Presidency. Her father wanted her to

Sarojini Naidu

Words to remember

orator: a person who is good at public speaking.
intellectual: a person who is well educated and enjoys activities in which they have to seriously think.
scholarship: an award of money to somebody to help pay for their education.
inter-caste: between two castes.
frail: physically weak or delicate.
enthuse: to make somebody feel very excited and interested.
***khadi*:** Indian handspun and hand-woven cloth.
coarse: rough or loose in texture.

become a mathematician or a scientist but she had a love for poetry from a very young age. Once while trying to solve an algebra problem, when she could not find its solution, she decided to take a break. In the same algebra book, she wrote, 'The Lady of the Lake', a 1,300-line long poem.

Sarojini had a flair for languages and was well versed in Urdu, Telugu, English, Persian and Bengali. Her father realized that she was more interested in poetry than in mathematics or science, so he decided to encourage her. He helped her in writing a play in the Persian language called *Maher Muneer*. The Nawab of Hyderabad was so impressed by it that he gave her a **scholarship** to study abroad. She got admitted to King's College of England at the age of sixteen.

At the age of nineteen, she married Dr Govindarajulu Naidu, whom she met in England. It was an **inter-caste** marriage and took place at a time when there were many restrictions on marrying a person of another caste. But her parents were broad-minded and gave their blessings. Her marriage was a very happy one and they had four children. They lived in a beautiful house which is now the city campus of the University of Hyderabad.

Her **frail** health did not let her continue with her higher studies. She travelled throughout Europe, read several art books and continued to write poetry.

The English authors, Arthur Simon and Edmond Gausse, whom Sarojini met in Europe, wanted her poems to be based on Indian settings like Indian rivers, mountains, valleys, temples and social background . Her poetry dealt with contemporary Indian life and events—snake charmers, beggars, fishermen, widows, bangle sellers, milkmaids, palanquin bearers, etc.

Her first collection of poems was published in 1905 under the title, *The Golden Threshold*.

She happened to be a good singer as well. This talent of hers fetched her the title 'Nightingale of India' or *Bulbul-e-Hind*. Later, *The Magic Tree*, *The Wizard Mask* and A *Treasury of Poems* were published. Her other published works were *The Bird of Time* (1912), *The Broken Wings* (1917) and *Feast of Youth* (1918).

Rabindranath Tagore and Jawaharlal Nehru were among the several admirers of her work. Though her poems had English words, they were purely Indian in spirit.

Sarojini with Mahatma Gandhi

Sarojini met Mahatma Gandhi in 1916, and became totally devoted to the cause of freedom. She travelled throughout the country like an army general and inspired the Indians to fight against the British. The freedom of India from the clutches of the British rule became her sole objective in life. Gopal Krishna Gokhale asked her to use her poetry to **enthuse** the villagers to fight for freedom of India. He asked her to use her gift of words to free her motherland. She became a follower of Gandhiji and accompanied him to Britain. In Britain, she openly criticized the British rule in India and soon became a centre of attraction among the intellectual group.

Sarojini brought the Indian women out of their kitchen and created an awareness and interest in them about the freedom struggle. She worked to free women from social and political restrictions. She travelled from place to place speaking up for the rights of women and helped to re-establish confidence and self-respect in them. She was in favour of all people, rich and poor, getting good education. She strongly supported Hindu-Muslim unity. She had good taste and was known for her fine collection of silks and jewellery. But for the sake of the national struggle, she gave up wearing fine clothes and wore only clothes made of **coarse *khadi***.

In 1916, under the influence of Jawaharlal Nehru, she started working for the cause of the indigo plantation workers of Champaran. In 1919, Naidu became the Home Rule League's ambassador to Britain and returned to India in July 1920. Sarojini Naidu was the first person to join to the Non-Cooperation Movement started by Mahatma Gandhi.

In 1925, she was elected President of the Indian National Congress in Kanpur, the first Indian woman to hold the post. In 1928, she went to the USA with the message of the non-violence movement. In 1930, when Gandhiji was arrested for a protest, she took charge of this movement. In 1931, she participated in the Round Table Conference, along with Gandhiji and Pandit Malaviyaji. In 1942, she was arrested during the Quit India Movement and stayed in jail for 21 months with Gandhiji.

Sarojini with Mahatma Gandhi in London for the Round Table Conference

When India became independent in 1947, she became the Governor of Uttar Pradesh. She was India's first woman governor and became known for her purity, courage, determination and self-confidence.

Sarojini Naidu became the first woman governor

Sarojini had a great sense of humour and was well known for her wit. She respected Gandhiji a lot but at the same time was close enough to joke with him.

She passed away on 2 March 1949 at Lucknow at the age of seventy, and India lost her *Bulbul*. Her name will always shine in the history of India as an inspiring poet and a daring freedom fighter.

Did you know?

The Sarojini Naidu Prize was instituted in 2001 for the best reporting on Women and Panchayati Raj. This prize is given every year to outstanding reporters to support the contribution of journalists to India's future.

Exercises

1. Answer the following.

(a) Who was Sarojini Naidu? When and where was she born?

(b) What were the themes of Sarojini Naidu's poetry?

(c) What was the main objective of Sarojini Naidu's life? How did she try to achieve it?

(d) What did Sarojini Naidu do for uplifting Indian women?

(e) Why was Naidu recognized as *Bulbul-e-Hind*?

2. Fill in the blanks.

(a) At the age of twelve, she topped her .... exams in the Madras Presidency.

(b) The ....gave her a scholarship to study abroad.

(c) In July 1919, Naidu became the ....ambassador to Britain.

(d) In 1925, she was elected as the .... of the Indian National Congress in Kanpur.

(e) She passed away at .... at the age of ....

3. Say whether the following are True or False.

(a) Sarojini's father wanted her to become a poet.

(b) In 1924, Naidu was arrested during the Quit India Movement and stayed in jail for 21 months with Gandhiji.

(c) When India became independent in 1947, she became the Chief Minister of Uttar Pradesh.

(d) Naidu was called *Bhartiya Kokila*.

(e) She wore clothes made of *khadi*.

Things to do

1. Complete the crossword.

Down

1. Sarojini's title
2. Her first collection
3. She studied here
4. She wrote this 1,300-line long poem

Across

5. Her play in Persian
6. Plantation workers

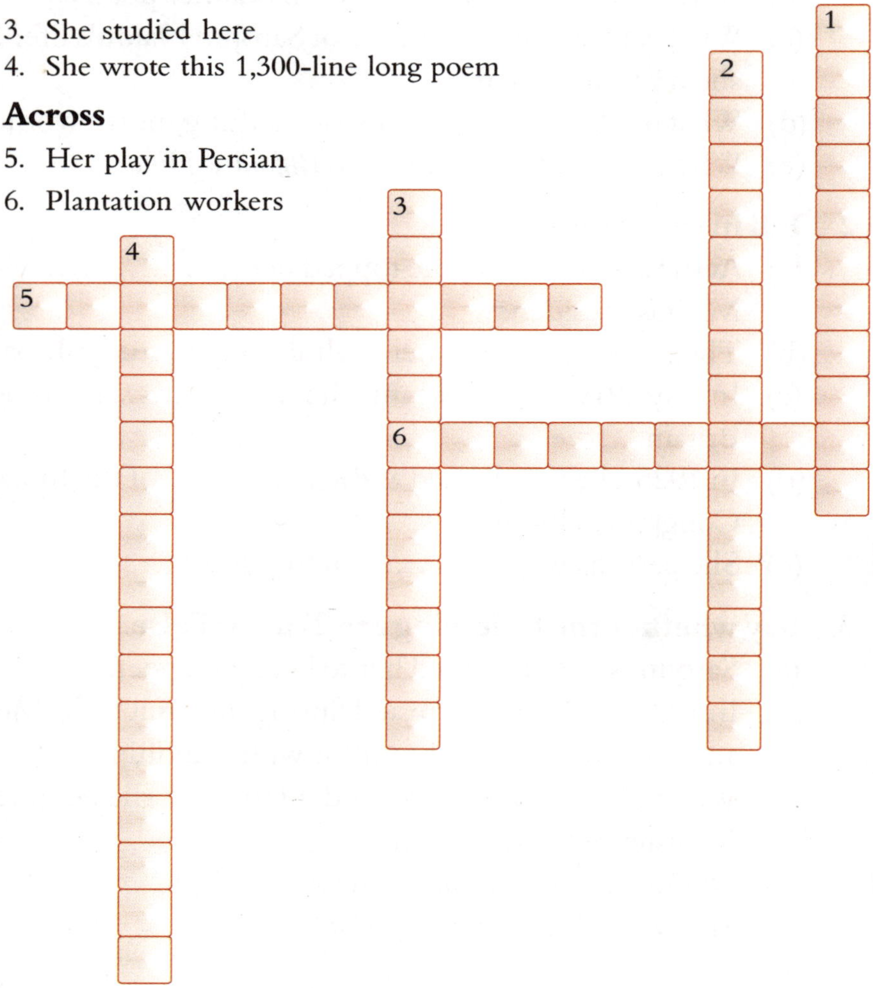

2. Find out!

Try and find some poems of Sarojini Naidu and recite them in class.

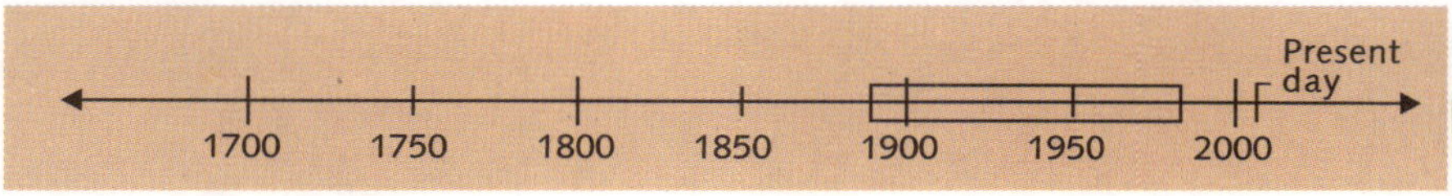

Mao Tse-tung

—The Chinese Communist leader

When Mao Tse-tung heard of Lenin and the great revolution in Russia, China was also passing through a time of suffering. In 1915, Japan had occupied the Shantung province of China. Confucius, the great Chinese thinker, had been born in Shantung. The Chinese regarded it as their Holy Land. Later in the same year, Japan sent a threatening letter to the Chinese president. Written on paper **watermarked** with machine guns, the letter demanded more areas in China and several Chinese ports. Japan

Mao Tse-tung

Words to remember

watermarked : symbol or design in some types of paper, which can be seen when the paper is held against the light.
swore : took an oath; made a serious promise to do something.
demonstration : a public meeting or march (often organized) protesting against or supporting somebody/something.
tramped : walked with heavy foot.
drenched : made wet all over.
frost : the thin white layer of ice that forms when the temperature drops below 0°C.
anniversary : yearly return of the date of an event.

An overhead view of the Square of Heavenly Peace as it looks now

wanted to command the police in the big Chinese cities, have Japanese officials in the Chinese government, and control the coal and iron mines and railways in China. The Japanese demands were supported by the powerful countries of Europe. The weak Chinese government had to accept these demands.

The Chinese people protested against giving in to Japan. There were banners at street corners reading, 'Don't forget the shame of the nation.' On 4 May 1919, over 3,000 students gathered at the Square of Heavenly Peace in Peking. They **swore** two oaths:

China's land may be conquered, but it cannot be given away.

The Chinese people may be killed, but they will not surrender.

Then they marched through the whole city. They distributed pamphlets protesting against the rulers. There were fights with the police at some places, and some students were arrested. The story of the 4 May **demonstration** spread to the other cities, and there were students' strikes and demonstrations all over China. In the province of Hunan, the students were led by Mao Tse-tung. Mao edited a student's journal, the *Hsiang Chiang Review*, and ran a bookshop at that time.

Mao Tse-tung was born in 1893. His father was a poor peasant. But he entered business and became quite rich. Mao went to school when he was eight. Early in the morning and at night he worked on the farm. During the day, he read the writings of Confucius. The Chinese teacher at school was very strict. He beat his students whenever he was angry. Mao's father also beat Mao and his brothers. Mao ran away from home when he was ten years old. He wandered for three days before his family found him. Mao had thought that he was walking towards the nearest city. But he had actually only gone round and round the same place. When he came back home, he found both his father and teacher more considerate. But his father still complained that young Mao was lazy and disobedient, and he sometimes beat the boy.

Mao left school for some time and worked long hours on the farm. At night he looked after his father's accounts. Still, he found time for reading. He loved to read old Chinese tales and stories of revolts in the past.

There was a great famine in China at the time. The hungry people went to the rich landlords and governors begging for food. When they were turned out, they often got angry and burnt down the houses of the rich. The leaders of these people were arrested. Their heads were cut off and hung upon poles to frighten the people. Mao was deeply moved by these events. He wanted to find out how the common people could be given a better life.

He went back to school to learn how things could be changed. Mao changed school a number of times. He found the schools teaching things in which he was not interested. He gave up going to school after a time and spent all his time reading in the Hunan Library. But Mao had no money. His father had refused to send him money unless he went to school. So he had to go to school again, where he studied hard.

In 1918, Mao passed out from school. He did not want to depend on his father any longer. He went to Peking and found a job as a library assistant at the University Library. He lived in a little room with seven other people. When they slept together there was little room for anyone to even turn over. Still, Mao was quite happy. He loved to watch the trees of Peking, and had lots of books to read in the library.

When he went up to college, he gathered a group of students around himself. It was a very serious-minded group of young people. They never talked about their personal problems or interests. They talked only of grand matters—of China and the world. They took great care to be strong and healthy. They **tramped** through the fields, up and down the mountains, and across the streams and rivers. They went out in the rain, took off their shirts and got **drenched**. They slept in the open when **frost** fell. In cold November, they swam in the rivers. This group grew into a society called the New People's Study Society.

Mao came back to Hunan in 1919. The students of the province learnt of the great students' demonstrations and strikes in 1919 all over China from Mao's journal, the *Hsiang Chiang Review*. The New People's Study Society organized students' strikes in Hunan. Soon Mao was leading the students who demanded independence for Hunan. They did not want to be ruled by the weak government in Peking.

The ideas of Karl Marx were just becoming known in China. Mao read Marx and was convinced that his ideas were right. He read about Lenin and the Russian Revolution. He felt that China, too, needed a revolution of the same kind. In 1920, the New People's Study Society held a demonstration on the third **anniversary** of the Russian Revolution. But the police broke up the meeting.

Mao realized that the students by themselves would not be able to do anything.

Marx had said that the workers should take a leading role in a revolution. So Mao brought workers into his society. In May 1921, followers of Marx's ideas met in Shanghai to form the Communist Party of China on the model of the Russian Bolshevik Party led by Lenin. They were inspired and guided by the ideas of Marx and Lenin. The new party was led by Mao Tse-tung from Hunan, Liu Shao-chi from Shanghai, Chou En-lai from Tientsin (modern Tianjin), and Chu Teh from Setzuan (Szechwan/Sichuan).

Dr Sun Yat-sen

Mao and the Communist Party reached an understanding with the other important political party of the day, the Kuomintang. Dr Sun Yat-sen, the leader of the Kuomintang, wanted China to have a government elected by the people and a better life for the poor. He insisted that the land on which crops were grown should be given to the man who tilled the field and raised the crops. The Communists supported Sun. The two parties together set up a revolutionary government at Canton and a military academy at Whampoa. The Russian government helped them with arms and military advisors.

Chiang Kai-shek

But Sun died in 1925. Chiang Kai-shek, the new leader of the Kuomintang, was determined to become the ruler of China. He made friends with the rich landlords, took large sums of money from them, and killed many Communists to please them. In 1928, Mao Tse-tung and Chu Teh formed the Red Army with 11,000 men. They set up their base in the Chingkang Mountains between Kiangsi and Hunan provinces. The valley could be reached only through five narrow passes. Almost the whole of Kiangsi province was soon being ruled by the Communist government at Chingkang. In this area, the peasants owned the land. Schools were set up to educate the poor people. In 1930 and 1931, Chiang attacked the Communist area four times, but his huge armies were defeated every time. The Red Army captured thousands of Kuomintang soldiers and thousands of rifles. In October 1933, Chiang surrounded the area with a million soldiers. Then his troops marched into the area. As it marched in, the circle became smaller and smaller. On their way, the Kuomintang soldiers burned crops, houses and animals, and killed thousands of people. In October 1934,

Did you know?

Mao wrote good poetry. He was also a skilled calligrapher with a highly personal style, and his calligraphy is still very visible in mainland China.

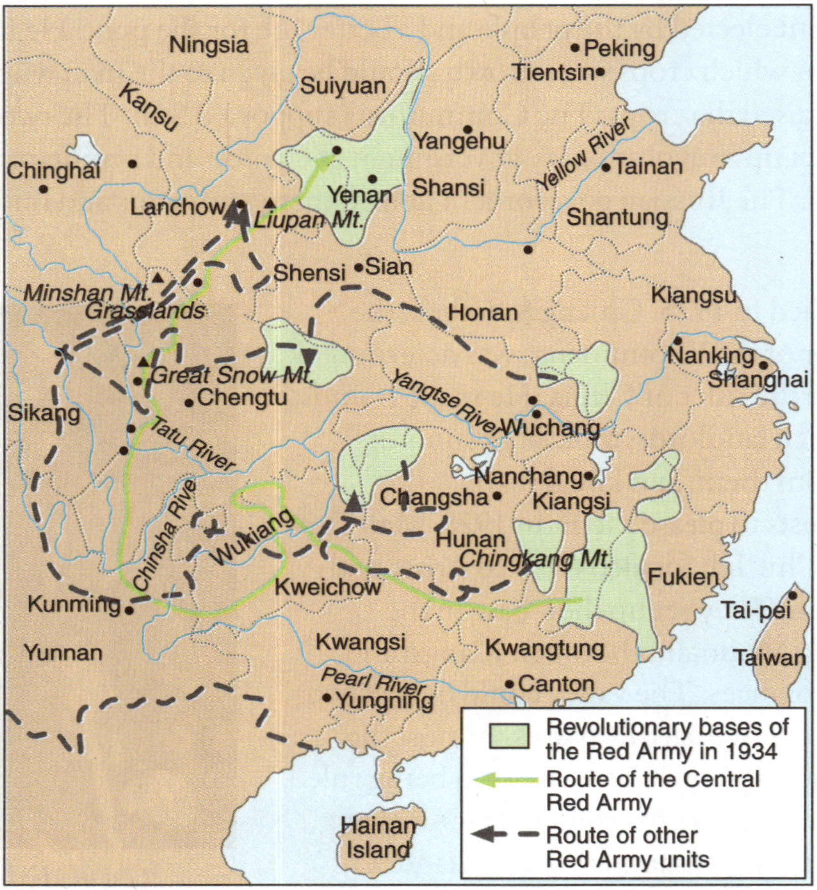

Route of the Long March

the Red Army with a million men and thirty-five women broke through the circle and started on the Long March to find a safe area for a new base. They marched over 10,000 kilometres and took a whole year to reach Yenan in Shensi province. On the way they crossed the dangerous Chinsha and Tatu Rivers, and the Great Snow Mountains. They marched through rain, hailstorm and biting cold. In a poem written during the Long March, Mao wrote:

The Red Army fears not the trials of a distant march;

To them a thousand mountains, ten thousand rivers are nothing.

Only 20,000 of the marchers reached Yenan, where they set up their new republic.

A photograph of soldiers on the Long March

From Yenan the Communists had to fight both the Kuomintang and the Japanese who had attacked China in 1931. In Yenan, they lived in caves. But they set up schools, hospitals and factories. They grew rice and cotton. They lived a simple life. The leaders and the ordinary people shared all the hardships alike. In 1947, the Kuomintang attacked them again in a big way. Yenan was destroyed. The Red Army broke up into small groups and attacked the Kuomintang at many places at the same time. Then, they spread out and took control of the whole of China.

Mao Tse-tung declaring the establishment of the People's Republic of China

In 1949, Mao and the Red Army finally defeated the Kuomintang army. Chiang and his followers fled to the island of Formosa. On 1 October 1949, Mao Tse-tung declared at a great parade in Peking, the establishment of the People's Republic of China. Mao became the first Chairman of the republic, and Chou, the first Prime Minister. Mao ruled China for 27 years till his death in 1976.

Exercises

1. Answer the following.

(a) What did Japan demand from China?

(b) How did the Chinese people protest against the surrender to Japan?
(c) How did the group of students try to be strong and healthy?
(d) What did Dr Sun Yat-sen want?
(e) How did Mao and his people make the Long March?

2. **Fill in the blanks.**
(a) Mao edited a journal called .... and ran a ....
(b) In .... the New People's Study Society held a demonstration on the third anniversary of the ....
(c) The new party was led by .... from Shanghai and .... from Setzuan.
(d) .... fled to the island of Formosa.
(e) .... became the first Prime Minister of the People's Republic of China.

3. **Say whether the following are True or False.**
(a) Dr Sun Yat-sen became the first chairman of the People's Republic of China.
(b) Mao was greatly influenced by Marx and Lenin.
(c) Confucius, the great Chinese thinker, had been born in Hunan.
(d) Dr Sun Yat-sen was the leader of the Kuomintang, before his death in 1925.
(e) Mao ruled China for 25 years till his death in 1970.

Things to do

1. **For your scrapbook.**

Collect pictures of Chinese people, villages, towns, paintings, etc. and paste them in your scrapbook.

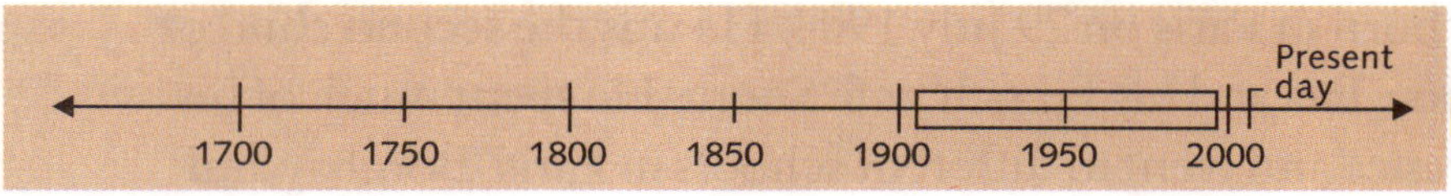

14

J.R.D. Tata

—The father of modern Indian industry

Jehangir Ratanji Dadabhoy Tata is probably India's most famous **industrialist**. He was known to the world as J.R.D., and to his friends as Jeh. He **inherited** his grandfather Jamshedji's industrial empire and his contribution to the development of Indian industry and **aviation** in particular, is enormous. He had great passion for flying, fast cars, skiing and literature.

J.R.D. Tata

Words to remember

industrialist: a person involved in the ownership and management of any branch of trade or manufacture.
inherited: receive as an heir at the death of the previous holder.
aviation: the activity of operating and flying aircraft.
regiment: a permanent unit of an army.
credited: to publicly recognize someone with some achievement or good quality.
diligent: hard-working.
enterprises: businesses or companies.
patronage: to give support and aid to someone.
poverty: the state of being poor; not having enough money even for basic needs.
avid: very keen and eager.

J.R.D. Tata was born in Paris on 29 July 1904. He was the second child of Ratanji Dadabhoy Tata and his French wife Sooni. He spent much of his childhood in France and went to different schools in Paris, Bombay and Yokohama. After finishing his school, J.R.D. joined the French army and was posted to a **regiment** in France called Le Saphis for a year. After this he wanted to go to the Cambridge University, but was called back to India by his father in 1922 to join the family business of the Tatas. In 1926, when his father died, J.R.D. Tata, who was then just twenty-one years old, became the director of the Board of Tata Sons Ltd, one of India's largest industrial groups.

J.R.D. loved flying

Although J.R.D. could not go to college, he studied books on his own on various aspects of business after office hours. Once when he was in his early twenties, and was recovering from typhoid, he came to his room, threw himself on the bed and started studying.

When his sister Rodabeh asked, 'Why don't you rest Jeh, you are tired and unwell,'

J.R.D. replied, 'I want to be worthy of Tatas.'

J.R.D. loved flying and was inspired by Louis Bleriot, the first person to fly across the English Channel. In 1929, he became the first Indian to get a pilot's licence.

When he was asked what was the greatest adventure of his life, he said, 'The flying experience. None can equal that.'

He further said, 'When you are on your own in that little plane at the control without an instructor, and the plane speeds on the runway and finally takes off—you know you are in the air on your own.'

He was later known as the Father of the Indian Civil Aviation. He founded India's first commercial airline, Tata Airlines in 1932, which became Air India in 1946, and is now India's international airline. J.R.D. Tata was the chairman of the Indian Airlines and Air India till 1978.

J.R.D. founded India's first airline

In 1938, at the age of thirty-four, he became the chairman of the Tata Group and held that post for 52 years. He was sincere and **diligent**. On being asked why he was made chairman at such a young age when other senior persons were there, he said, 'Perhaps, because I was hard-working.'

The Tatas started several new **enterprises** under J.R.D.'s leadership from airlines to hotels, trucks to locomotives, heavy chemicals to pharmaceuticals and financial services, tea and air-conditioning to cosmetics. The group tried to make everything and do everything. J.R.D. strengthened the existing businesses such as steel, power, hotels, engineering and several other industries. In 1945, under the able guidance of J.R.D., Tata Steel set up the Tata Engineering and Locomotive Company (TELCO) to produce locomotives for the Indian Railways. Telco is ranked today as India's largest commercial vehicle manufacturer. J.R.D. with his enterprising skills is rightly **credited** with placing the Tata Group on the world map.

J.R.D. Tata was a great patron of arts and was highly respected by Indian artists, sculptors and performing artists. Under his **patronage**, the Tatas became the biggest buyers and supporters of the art world in India. He also encouraged sporting talent in India and was responsible for starting the Cricket Club of India. He also founded many famous educational institutions in India.

J.R.D. was also a very sensitive person and was moved by the **poverty** he saw around him and made tremendous efforts to improve the condition of the poor. As a step towards this, he built up Tata charitable trusts. He wanted the people to be happy and did all he could to make them so.

J.R.D. spent a good deal of his time in his study. He had an entire shelf of books on aviation, another on military ventures and warfare, and one on sports cars and motor racing. He was an **avid** reader and liked to read crime fiction.

The success of the Tatas is largely due to the support of its workforce. Tata Steel was one of the earliest companies in India to have a special department to look after the welfare of its workers. J.R.D. felt that each person should be dealt in his own way and the best in people should be brought out. He would say, 'At times, it involved suppressing yourself. It is painful but necessary... To lead men, you have to lead them with affection.' He had great respect for people and genuinely cared for them. People also loved and admired him a lot.

Kalpana Chawla, the Indian-born astronaut who died in the *Columbia* space shuttle disaster, considered J.R.D. and his pioneering airmail flights to be her inspiration for taking up aeronautics. He touched the lives of countless others, rich and poor, and manager and worker.

During his lifetime J.R.D. Tata received several awards. In 1957, he received the *Padma Vibhushan* on the eve of silver jubilee of Air India. He received the Guggenheim Medal for aviation in 1988. He was awarded the *Bharat Ratna* in 1992 for his contribution to industry and nation building.

President R. Venkataraman conferring the Bharat Ratna on J.R.D. Tata

On being told that the Indian government was thinking about giving him the *Bharat Ratna*, the country's highest civilian award, he is reported to have said, 'Why me? I don't deserve it. The *Bharat Ratna* is usually given to people who are dead or it is given to politicians. I am not prepared to oblige the government on the former and I am not the latter.'

Did you know?

J.R.D. was a weightlifter and a great fitness freak. Even at the age of sixty, he could do fifty push-ups!

In 1992, he also received the United Nations Population Award. In 1991, at the age of eighty-seven, J.R.D. Tata retired from Tata Sons.

He died on 29 November 1993 in Geneva, Switzerland at the age of eighty-nine and India lost one of her most precious people.

Exercises

1. Answer the following questions.

(a) Why did J.R.D. Tata visit France so often in his young days? Why was he not able to continue with his college education?

(b) Why was J.R.D. known as the Father of Indian Civil Aviation?

(c) What were the different businesses of the Tatas under the leadership of J.R.D. Tata?

(d) What were the different interests that J.R.D. pursued?

(e) What was J.R.D.'s reaction on being told that the government was considering him for the *Bharat Ratna*?

2. Fill in the blanks.

(a) Le Saphis is an army .... in France.

(b) J.R.D. went to different .... in Paris, Bombay and Yokohama.

(c) Tata Steel set up the Tata Engineering and Locomotive Company to produce .... for the Indian Railways.

(d) J.R.D. died on 29 November in.........

3. Match the following.

(a) Jamshedji	India's international airline
(b) Guggenheim Medal	J.R.D.'s sister
(c) Air India	J.R.D.'s mother
(d) Rodabeh	J.R.D.'s grandfather
(e) Sooni	For aviation

Things to do

1. Prepare a report.

In groups of five or six prepare a report on the industries or businesses that the Tatas are associated with.

2. In the grid on the next page, eight words related to this chapter are arranged vertically, horizontally and diagonally. Fill in the blanks using the words from the grid.

(a) J.R.D. Tata was a well-known ....

(b) J.R.D. was a pioneer in ....

(c) .... was the first person to fly across the English Channel.

(d) J.R.D. Tata wanted to go to .... University for higher studies.

(e) J.R.D. Tata died in ....

(f) His friends called him ……………….. .

(g) He spent most of his childhood in ……………….. .

(h) ……………….. is ranked toady as India's largest vehicle manufacturer.

M	A	I	N	T	A	C	A	S	C	T	A
T	K	N	A	V	I	A	T	I	O	N	R
U	L	D	D	R	T	M	I	H	M	B	Q
B	O	U	A	Z	G	B	A	J	B	U	P
G	Q	S	B	L	E	R	I	O	T	A	S
E	F	T	O	D	N	I	R	O	I	I	T
N	T	R	K	X	E	D	D	F	D	Y	I
K	A	I	A	U	V	G	S	O	G	A	N
F	U	A	M	N	A	E	N	C	E	H	U
R	G	I	Y	Z	C	A	D	G	I	B	S
A	H	S	J	N	J	E	H	I	L	Y	T
T	P	T	E	L	C	O	R	P	B	X	A
E	C	G	V	A	B	J	R	M	O	T	L

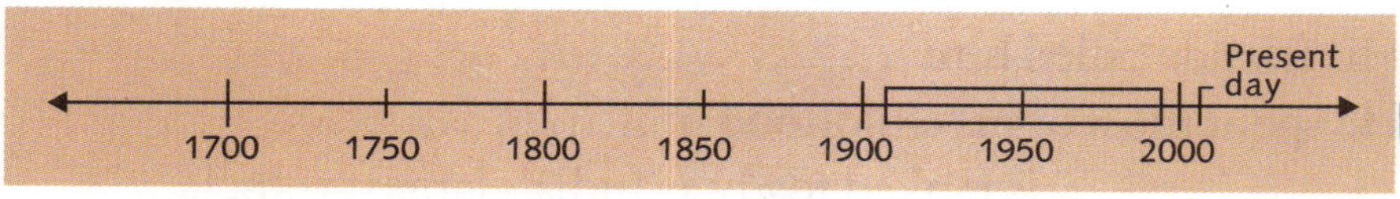

Mother Teresa

—The angel of mercy

Mother Teresa was born in 1910 in Skopje in Albania (now in the Republic of Macedonia). Daughter of an Albanian grocer, she was named Agnes Gonxha Bojaxhiu. At an early age, young Agnes felt the call to help others. As a public school student, she developed a special interest in overseas missions and helping the poor.

Mother Teresa

Words to remember

missionaries : people who are sent to a foreign country to teach about Christianity.

patroness : a female person who supports an organization, such as charity.

catechism : teachings about the beliefs of the Christian religion.

order : a group of people living in a religious community.

hospice : a hospital for people who are dying.

summoned : called in.

humanitarian : concerned with reducing the suffering and improving the living conditions.

unanimous : a decision agreed by everyone in a group.

beatified : to give a dead person a special honour by stating officially that he or she is very holy.

When she was eighteen years old, she went to Ireland to join the Sisters of Loretto, a community of Irish nuns. She was inspired to work in India by reports sent from **missionaries** in Bengal. After spending six weeks in Ireland, she sailed to India as a teacher. There, she took the name 'Sister Teresa', after Saint Teresa of Lisieux, the **patroness** of missionaries.

From 1930 to 1948, Mother Teresa taught geography and **catechism** at St Mary's High School in Calcutta and became its Principal in 1944. The poverty and the presence of the sick and dying on the streets of Calcutta deeply moved her and their pathetic condition touched her heart.

In September 1946, something happened that changed her life forever. Mother Teresa had fallen ill and was suspected to be suffering from tuberculosis. She was sent to Darjeeling to recover. While travelling in a train, she received a calling from God to give up everything that she was doing. She was ordered to follow Him to the slums and serve Him among the poorest of the poor. After this incident, she said, 'I see God in every human being. When I wash the leper's wounds, I feel I am nursing the Lord himself. Is it not a beautiful experience?'

She requested the Pope to allow her to leave the **order** and live as an independent nun. Two years later, she received the permission from Pope Pius XII, through the Archbishop of Calcutta. She quit the school and did a short course with the Medical Mission Sisters in Patna.

When she returned to Calcutta, she started an open-air school for homeless children. Soon her former pupils and others joined her, who wanted to give her a helping hand. She also received financial support from the church and the municipal authorities. In this way, she could arrange for dispensaries and outdoor schools.

In October 1950, Teresa received permission from the Vatican to start her own order, which came to be known as the 'Missionaries of Charity'. Mother Teresa proclaimed that its mission was to care for 'the hungry, the naked, the homeless, the crippled, the blind, the lepers, all those people who feel unwanted, unloved, uncared for in society, people who have become a burden to society and are shunned by everyone.'

Mother Teresa found men, women, and children dying on the streets, who were rejected by local hospitals. The group rented a room so that they could care for the helpless people who would otherwise have died a painful death due to the negligence of society. The municipal authorities gave her a pilgrim hostel on her request, near the sacred temple of Kali.

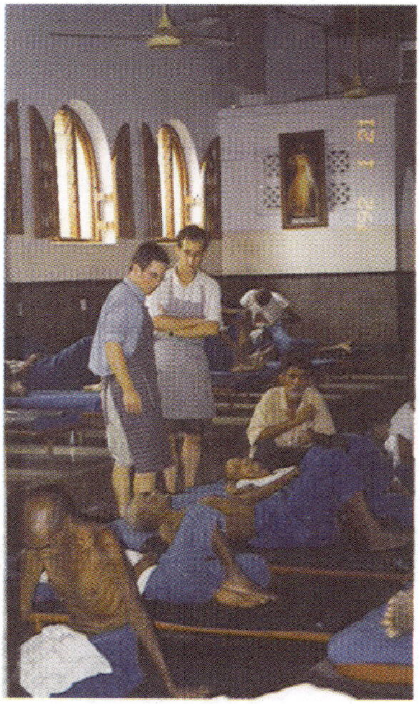

Volunteers at Nirmal Hriday

In 1952, she established Nirmal Hriday ('Pure Heart'), a **hospice** where the terminally ill could die with dignity. Her order also opened numerous centres serving the blind, the aged, and the disabled. Under Mother Teresa's guidance, the Missionaries of Charity built a leper colony, called Shanti Nagar (Town of Peace) near Asansol.

In 1963, the Indian government awarded Mother Teresa the title *Padmashri* for her services to the people of India. In 1964, on his trip to India, Pope Paul VI gave her his ceremonial limousine. Mother Teresa immediately sold the limousine to help finance her leper colony.

Pope John Paul II and Mother

In 1965, by granting a Decree of Praise, Pope Paul VI granted Mother Teresa's request to expand her order to other countries. Her order started to grow rapidly, with new shelters opening all over the world. The order's first house outside India was in Venezuela, and others followed in Rome and Tanzania, and eventually in many countries in Asia, Africa, and Europe, including Albania. In addition, the first Missionaries of Charity home in the United States was established in South Bronx, New York.

In 1968, she was **summoned** to Rome to set up a home there, to be staffed with Indian nuns. In recognition of her apostle, she was honoured by the Pope on 6 January 1971, with the first Pope John XXIII Peace Prize.

In 1979, she received the Nobel Peace Prize for her **humanitarian** work. She accepted the Nobel Peace Prize in the name of the 'unwanted, unloved and uncared for'.

Mother Teresa receiving the Nobel Prize

In her later years, Mother Teresa suffered ill health and had a heart attack in 1989. In 1990, she resigned as head of the order but was returned to office by a near **unanimous** vote. The lone vote against her was her own. Her worsening heart condition forced her to retire, and on 13 March 1997, she stepped down from the head of Missionaries of Charity and the order chose Sister Nirmala as her successor. Mother Teresa died on 5 September 1997, just 9 days after her 87th birthday.

At the time of Mother Teresa's death, the Missionaries of Charity, which had begun with only ten members, had around 4,000 nuns and one million workers in 517 missions providing service in more than 100 countries. Perhaps French President Jacques Chirac summed up her legacy best when he said after her death, 'This evening, there is less love, less compassion, less light in the world.' Within two years of Mother Teresa's death, the process to declare her a saint started. She was **beatified** on 19 October 2003, reaching the ranks of the blessed in the shortest time in the history of the church.

She had once said 'The other day I dreamt that I was at the gates of heaven ... and St Peter said, 'Go back to Earth, there are no slums up here.' Today, mankind requires many more like her to help the needy and the homeless.

Did you know?

In 1982, she persuaded the Israelis and Palestinians, who were in the midst of a skirmish, to cease fire long enough so that she could rescue the 37 mentally challenged patients trapped in a hospital in Beirut.

Exercises

1. Answer the following.

(a) Who was Mother Teresa?

(b) Why did Mother Teresa come to India? What touched her heart deeply?

(c) Describe the incident that took place in 1946 which changed Mother Teresa's life forever.

(d) What is the Missionaries of Charity? What is its mission?

(e) Why was Mother Teresa given the title *Padmashri*?

2. Fill in the blanks.

(a) Mother Teresa was born in the year ....

(b) In 1979, Teresa received the Nobel Peace Prize for her .... work.

(c) In 1964, on his trip to India, Pope Paul VI gave Teresa his ceremonial ....

(d) In October 1950, Teresa received .... permission to start her own order in Calcutta.

(e) Mother Teresa was .... on 19 October 2003, reaching the ranks of the blessed in the .... time in the history of the church.

3. **Match the following.**

(a) *Nirmal Hriday*	Patna
(b) Shanti Nagar	Leper colony
(c) Sister Nirmala	Pure Heart
(d) Medical Mission Sisters	Successor of Mother Teresa

Things to do

1. **Find out.**
   Visit a slum cluster with your parents in your neighbourhood. Write down your observations. What can you do to improve the condition of the people living there?

2. **Character study.**
   Draw a character sketch of Mother Teresa and share it in your class.

3. **Check out the following website for some quotations.**
   http://www.brainyquote.com/quotes/mother (accessed on 11 August 06)
   http://www.ewtn.com/motherteresa/words (accessed on 11 August 06)

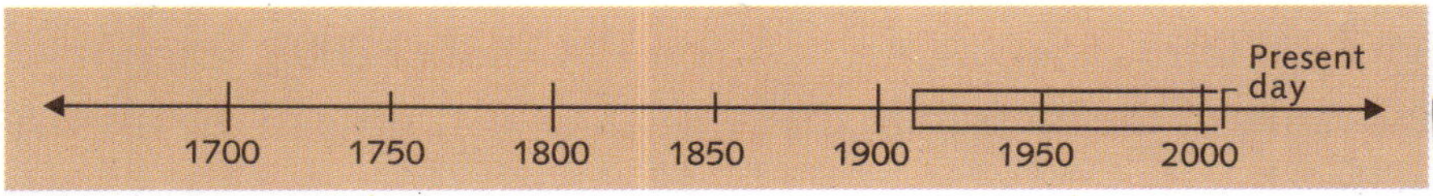

Nelson Mandela

—The man who battled apartheid

The Republic of South Africa is the southernmost country in the African continent. For many years, the black native people of South Africa were **discriminated against** by the white colonialists. As late as 1994, a **vicious** form of official **racism** called apartheid divided the people of South Africa.

Apartheid means 'separateness' in Afrikaans, which is one of the official languages of South Africa. Through apartheid, almost all the power and wealth of the country were in the hands of the white minority, while the black majority was powerless and suffered from poverty. The right of the black people to own land was limited, and in most parts of South Africa, they could not vote. There were laws which divided South Africans into racial groups — 'white', 'Indian', 'native' and coloured'. Power and wealth remained in the hands of the white people, who were a minority.

It was Nelson Mandela, who waged a battle to bring the hated system of apartheid to an end. A boy from an African village, he grew up to

Words to remember

discriminated against : treated somebody less fairly than others.
vicious : violent and cruel.
racism : the unfair treatment of people who belong to a different race.
renounced : gave up.
atrocities : terrible, violent and cruel acts.
remission : reduction in the amount of time spent in prison.

become the world's most famous political prisoner who spent 27 years in prison for struggling against this unfair system.

Nelson Mandela

Nelson was born on 18 July 1918, in Mvezo, a village in the Transkei region of South Africa. He was the son of a chief of the Tembu tribe and was groomed to be a chief. His parents named him Rolihlahla in Afrikaans, which means 'troublemaker'. Little did they know that their troublemaker son would lead a struggle against apartheid and become the first black President of the Republic of South Africa.

Nelson Mandela at the age of nineteen

At school, he was given the English name Nelson. He **renounced** his claim to the chieftainship to become a lawyer. He attended the University College of Fort Hare and studied law at the University of Witwatersrand. He later passed the qualification exam and became a lawyer. In 1952, he opened the first black legal firm in the country with his friend, Oliver Tambo. As legal practitioners, they came across thousands of stories of injustices of apartheid and **atrocities** of the government. Though they had risen to professional status in their community, every case, every visit to the prison to interview clients reminded them of the humiliation and suffering of the people.

Mandela was opposed to the cruel and unfair system of apartheid. He joined the African National Congress (ANC) in 1944, a political organization that opposed the ruling National Party's apartheid policies after 1948. The ANC believed that South Africa belonged to all of her people, whatever their colour.

Nelson Mandela was a natural leader and a gifted speaker. He became the Deputy President of the ANC and encouraged people to break the government's apartheid laws. The government saw him as a troublemaker and tried to stop him. The ANC was made illegal and Mandela was arrested several times. After the banning of the ANC in 1960, Nelson Mandela argued for the setting up of a military wing within the ANC. In June 1961, the ANC executive considered his proposal on the use of violent tactics and agreed that those members who wished to involve themselves in Mandela's campaign would not be stopped from doing so by the ANC. This led to the formation of Umkhonto we Sizwe.

In 1962, Mandela left the country for military training in Algeria and to arrange training for other members. He was again arrested in 1962 and sentenced to five years' imprisonment with hard labour. In 1963, when the leaders of the ANC and other parties were arrested, Mandela was also brought to stand trial with them for plotting to overthrow the government. His statements received considerable international publicity.

On 12 June 1964, eight of the accused, including Mandela, were sentenced to life imprisonment. In his closing statement during the trial he said:

> *'During my lifetime I have dedicated myself to this struggle of the African people. I have fought against white domination, and I have fought against black domination. I have cherished the ideal of a democratic and free society in which all persons live together in harmony and with equal opportunities. It is an ideal which I hope to live for and to achieve. But if needs be, it is an ideal for which I am prepared to die.'*

From 1964 to 1982, he was imprisoned at Robben Island prison, off Cape Town. Conditions were harsh in the prison, and he was allowed only one visitor every six months. He consistently refused to change his political stand to obtain his freedom. During the seventies, he refused the offer of a **remission** of sentence if he returned to Transkei and settled there. In the eighties, he again rejected the offer of freedom if he renounced violence.

Robben Island, where he was imprisoned, became a centre for learning, and Mandela was a central figure in conducting the political education classes. In prison, Mandela stood firmly by his political principles and was always a source of strength for the other prisoners.

In 1982, the government sent him to Pollsmoor prison, which was on the mainland. This was a time marked by violence in South Africa, with street protests against apartheid. The government began secret talks with Mandela, knowing that if anyone could stop the trouble, it was Mandela, because of the mass support he had from the South Africans.

Mandela was kept at Pollsmoor prison till 1990. He became the world's most famous political prisoner. People from all over the world wanted him to be freed, and that apartheid be put to an end in South Africa. He was widely accepted as the most significant black leader in South Africa and became a potent symbol of resistance as the anti-apartheid movement gathered strength.

On 11 February 1990, the then South Africa's President, F.W. de Klerk, released Mandela after 27 years in prison. The ban on the ANC was lifted. It is significant that shortly after his release, Mandela and his delegation agreed to end armed struggle. In 1991, the first national conference of the ANC was held inside South Africa after the organization had been banned in 1960. Mandela was elected the President of the ANC while his lifelong friend and colleague, Oliver Tambo, became the organization's National Chairperson.

Nelson Mandela receiving the Nobel Peace Prize

In 1993, he was awarded the Nobel Peace Prize. While accepting the prize, he said, 'We stand here today as nothing more than a representative of the millions of our people who dared to rise up against a social system whose very essence is war, violence, racism, oppression, repression and the impoverishment of an entire people.'

In April 1994, a general election was held in which, for the first time, men and women of all races and all colours could vote. The ANC won, and Nelson Mandela became the first black President of South Africa. He brought an end to the much hated apartheid system.

Nelson Mandela is a great admirer of Mahatma Gandhi and his unique non-violent struggle for freedom. While he was preparing for his release, he was helped by the biography of Pandit Nehru, who wrote of what happened when one left the jail. Nelson Mandela's writings and speeches are collected in *No Easy Walk to Freedom* and *I Am Prepared to Die*. He published his autobiography *Long Walk to Freedom* in 1994.

His daughter, Zinzi, says that she grew up without a father, who, when he returned, became a father of the nation. This placed a great responsibility on his shoulders. Nelson Mandela retired from active politics in 1999. He now lives in the Transkei region, where he had spent his childhood.

Nelson Mandela played a pivotal role in the removal of apartheid from this world, which was possible only due to his self-sacrifice. In South Africa, everyone now has an equal opportunity in all walks of life and there is no discrimination on the basis of colour or creed.

Did you know?

In 1990, Nelson Mandela was awarded the *Bharat Ratna*, which is India's highest civilian award.

Exercises

1. **Answer the following.**
   (a) When and where was Nelson Mandela born?
   (b) What is apartheid? How did it divide the people of South Africa?

(c) What is ANC? Why did Mandela join the ANC?
(d) Why was Nelson Mandela awarded the Nobel Peace Prize?
(e) How did Nelson Mandela become the first black President of South Africa?

2. Fill in the blanks.

(a) For many years, the .... people of South Africa were discriminated against by the white colonialists.
(b) Mandela's parents named him .... in Afrikaans, which means ....
(c) Apartheid means .... in Afrikaans, which is one of the official languages of ....
(d) Nelson Mandela is a great admirer of .... and his unique non-violent struggle for freedom.
(e) Mandela was kept at .... prison till 1990.

3. Give one word answer.

(a) The prison, which became a centre for learning and where Mandela conducted political education classes
(b) Mandela's lifelong friend and colleague, who became ANC's National Chairperson
(c) Mandela's daughter
(d) The number of years that Mandela spent in jail as a political prisoner

Things to do

1. Map work.
On a map of Africa, mark the places that have been mentioned in this chapter.

2. Find out.
Can you find some similarities between Nelson Mandela and Mahatma Gandhi? Discuss in class.

Unit Test 2

Maximum Marks: 15

1. Give one word for the following. ½×6=3

(a) A person who fights against or refuses to serve the established government

(b) Small single pages usually containing information on a specific subject expressing political or religious opinion

(c) Symbol or design in some types of paper, which can be seen when the paper is held against light

(d) Concerned with reducing the suffering and improving the living conditions

(e) A decision agreed upon by everyone in the group

(f) The unfair treatment of people who belong to a different race

2. Answer the following. 1×6=6

(a) How did Sarojini Naidu try to help women in India?

(b) How did Gandhiji help the untouchables?

(c) Who was Karl Marx? What did he ask his followers to do?

(d) Give one example to show that Winston Churchill was brave and courageous.

(e) What is the most important objective of the Missionaries of Charity?

(f) What do you understand by the term 'apartheid'?

3. Fill in the blanks. ½×6=3

(a) The Russian emperor was known as the ..... .

(b) Winston Churchill is affectionately remembered as the ....

(c) .... was known as the Father of Indian Civil Airation.

(d) The Communist Party was inspired by the ideas of ….. and …….. .

(e) .... was the first black President of South Africa.

4. Say whether the following statements are True or False. ½×6 = 3

(a) Sarojini Naidu became the governor of Madhya Pradesh.

(b) Gandhiji believed that freedom could be won only through violence.

(c) Churchill received the Nobel Prize for literature.

(d) J.R.D. Tata went to Cambridge for higher studies.

(e) Chiang Kai-shek was the leader of the Chinese Communist Party.

(f) Nelson Mandela spent twenty years in prison.